SIDREA Series in Accounting and Business Administration

Mauro Paoloni, University of Rome Tor Vergata, Rome, Italy

Paola Paoloni, University of Rome Tor Vergata, Rome, Italy, Sapienza University of Rome, Rome, Italy

Marcantonio Ruisi, University of Palermo, Palermo, Italy

Claudio Teodori, University of Brescia, Brescia, Italy

Simone Terzani, University of Perugia, Perugia, Italy

Stefania Veltri, University of Calabria, Rende, Italy

This is the official book series of SIDREA - the Italian Society of Accounting and Business Administration. This book series is provided with a wide Scientific Committee composed of Academics by SIDREA. It publishes contributions (monographs, edited volumes and proceedings) as a result of the double blind review process by the SIDREA's thematic research groups, operating at the national and international levels. Particularly, the series aims to disseminate specialized findings on several topics – classical and cutting-edge alike – that are currently being discussed by the accounting and business administration communities. The series authors are respected researchers and professors in the fields of business valuation; governance and internal control; financial accounting; public accounting; management control; gender; turnaround predictive models; non-financial disclosure; intellectual capital, smart technologies, and digitalization; and university governance and performance measurement.

Alessandro Gabrielli

Tax Avoidance and Capital Structure

Empirical Evidence on Debt Covenants

 Springer

Alessandro Gabrielli
University of Pisa
Pisa, Italy

ISSN 2662-9879 ISSN 2662-9887 (electronic)
SIDREA Series in Accounting and Business Administration
ISBN 978-3-031-30979-3 ISBN 978-3-031-30980-9 (eBook)
https://doi.org/10.1007/978-3-031-30980-9

This Springer imprint is published by the registered company Springer Nature Switzerland AG
The registered company address is: Gewerbestrasse 11, 6330 Cham, Switzerland

Preface

Tax avoidance has been a crucial issue for governments to address for decades, fuelling an intense debate among both practitioners and scholars.[1] Tax Justice Network reports that countries are losing more than US$427 billion each year due to aggressive corporate tax avoidance practices, as well as from tax evasion by wealthy private individuals. Urged by these numbers, several important cases of large corporations' tax avoidance have been covered by the media in recent years, drawing an increasing attention from the public on the topic. For example, Amazon was accused of tax dodging for having used tax losses to shield the taxable income of European affiliates.[2] Similarly, Google was accused of taking advantage of the "double-Irish" tax arrangement to shift more than $74.5 billion in profits out of Ireland.[3] Other notable tax scandals also emerged from the Panama Papers and, more recently, by the Pandora Papers.[4]

It is a common stand that tax avoidance may severely threat a government's revenues and its budgetary spending potential, as it reduces public investments for infrastructures and other essential services.[5] However, tax avoidance—especially in its legal and benign forms—can also be a relevant source of funding for many businesses, preserving them from failing and, ultimately, allowing them to continue to operate as going concern. In the recent efforts to cope with the coronavirus Covid-

---

[1] See: https://www.oecd.org/ctp/fightingtaxevasion.htm

[2] See: https://www.internationaltaxreview.com/article/b1rqp7jwn504jz/this-week-in-tax-amazons-tax-filings-reignite-tax-avoidance-debate

[3] See: https://www.irishtimes.com/business/technology/google-used-double-irish-to-shift-75-4bn-in-profits-out-of-ireland-1.4540519

[4] See e.g.: https://www.icij.org/investigations/panama-papers/; https://www.icij.org/investigations/pandora-papers/

[5] When multinational corporations abuse their tax responsibility to society, they weaken the supports that our economies need to work and create wealth. (Alex Cobham, Chief executive of Tax Justice Network, as reported by the Guardian: https://www.theguardian.com/business/2019/dec/02/new-study-deems-amazon-worst-for-aggressive-tax-avoidance)

19 economic crisis, missing tax payments due to tax avoidance can be a significant concern for governments aimed at stimulating economic recovery and relief after the pandemic.[6] At the same time, however, cash tax benefits can be useful for firms to create precautionary savings which, in turn, can help them, and eventually the State, to avoid the negative economic and societal consequences related to corporate liquidations and financial disruptions. Not surprisingly, many regulators have enacted several policy interventions intended to facilitate corporate reorganizations and early restructurings, by allowing financially troubled firms to obtain substantial tax benefits. Remarkable, for example, is the recent US Coronavirus Aid, Relief, and Economic Security Act (a.k.a., CARES Act) which has removed some of the limitations on the use and availability of net operating losses for tax purposes, as previously set by the 2017 Tax Cuts and Jobs Act (a.k.a., "Trump Reform"), to bring relief and promoting economic recovery after the Covid-19 crisis.

This monograph reviews the academic literature examining how tax avoidance is used by firms as a potential source of financing and its implications for a firm's capital structure, once agency conflicts pertaining to such activities are considered. The book, then, explores the changing nature of agency conflicts along the life cycle stages of a firm and the key role that debt covenants play within the corporate capital structure management. Drawing on the Agency Theory and on the life cycle theory, the research also elaborates a set of original hypotheses relating the effect of tax avoidance on the debt covenant violation likelihood for each stage of the corporate life cycle. Using quantitative research methods, the study provides empirical evidence at support of its hypotheses. The findings suggest that motivation and aims of corporate tax avoidance activities change across a firm's life cycle, as the result of a different level of alignment of interests between the bondholders, the shareholders (and the managers), resulting in different debt covenant violation probabilities. The monograph ends with final remarks, suggesting potential avenues for future research.

This study can be of interest for both experienced and early-stage scholars interested in the topic. The research can also offer matters for reflections for policymakers, investors, analysts, lenders, and other market participants. Overall, this book can offer valuable insights into how tax avoidance is used by firms as a source of financing. The research highlights the role of different, and often competing, stakeholders' motivations in shaping tax avoidance activities, as well as in directing the use of the resources retrieved from such practices.

Pisa, Italy   Alessandro Gabrielli

---

[6] See e.g.: https://www.washingtonpost.com/us-policy/2020/11/19/global-tax-evasion-data/

Acknowledgments

I am grateful to Prof. Giulio Greco (University of Pisa) and to Prof. Marco Maria Mattei (University of Bologna) for providing helpful comments. Alessandro Gabrielli gratefully acknowledges financial support from the Department of Economics and Management at the University of Pisa. All errors and omissions are sole responsibility of the author.

Contents

Chapter 1
Introduction

Keywords Tax avoidance · Agency conflicts · Capital structure · Debt covenants · Corporate life cycle

This book provides a comprehensive overview of the implications of tax avoidance for the corporate capital structure, providing original empirical evidence on the effect of tax avoidance activities for the debt covenant violation likelihood at each stage of a firm's life cycle. Covenants are crucial features of debt agreements of many firms and play a critical role within the corporate capital structure management (Dichev & Skinner, 2002; Demerjian & Owens, 2016). The Agency theory suggests that, by writing covenants in debt contracts, the managers implicitly make the promise to avoid harmful discretion towards the lenders, promoting actions that are expected maximize their net benefit (Jensen & Meckling, 1976; Myers, 1977; Smith & Warner, 1979). In this sense, the violation of a debt covenant can represent a highly costly event for the firm, which can exacerbate existing agency conflicts, increasing the firm's cost-of-capital and the related risk of financial default. (Gao et al., 2017; Roberts & Sufi, 2009; Freudenberg et al., 2017) Prior literature suggests that firms may engage accounting discretion and other "window dressing" activities to reduce the debt covenant violation likelihood and avoiding undesired increases of the firm's cost-of-capital (e.g., Dyreng et al., 2022). Tax avoidance is likely to complement the set of strategies available to the managers to avoid or delay covenant violation, hijacking much needed resources from the state to the company (Kim et al., 2010). However, tax avoidance is not a simple transfer of resources from the state to the firm and its shareholders because of agency conflicts afflicting the managers-shareholders and bondholders' relationship (Desai & Dharmapala, 2009). Therefore, the underlaying agency conflicts are likely to condition the relationship between tax avoidance and debt covenant violation.

According to a first strand of the academic literature, tax avoidance may be viewed as an alternative source of financing through which firms could replace other more expensive external sources of funds (e.g., Kim et al., 2010; Guenther et al., 2020; Lee et al., 2022; Edwards et al., 2016; Dhawan et al., 2020). Previous studies find that tax avoidance is negatively associated with a firm's level of indebtment, consistent with a tax avoidance-debt substitution effect (DeAngelo &

Masulis, 1980; MacKie-Mason, 1990; Graham & Tucker, 2006; Lim, 2011a; Lin et al., 2014; De Vito & Jacob, 2021; Lee et al., 2022). If tax avoidance is used by firms as a substitute for debt, then—according to this view—a higher level of tax avoidance is likely to reduce the firm's risk of financial default, consistent with a prevailing value-increasing effect (Kim et al., 2010; Lim, 2011b; Lin et al., 2014; Alexander et al., 2017). Kim et al. (2010), for example, suggest that tax avoidance impacts on both priced and non-priced terms of bank loans. Aggressive tax avoider firms exhibit fewer covenants' restrictions and have, on average, a lower likelihood to incur violation, consistent with tax avoidance being a credit quality enhancing tool. However, such a conclusion might be only partial if the agency costs pertaining to corporate capital structure decisions—including firm's tax avoidance decisions—are not considered (Jensen & Meckling, 1976; Desai & Dharmapala, 2009).

Agency conflicts arise all the time in which two or more cooperating parties have different goals and a different set of information (Jensen & Meckling, 1976; Eisenhardt, 1989). Morellec et al. (2012, p. 803) argue that the capital structure of a firm is determined "*not only by market frictions such as taxes, bankruptcy costs, or refinancing costs, but also by the severity of manager-shareholder conflicts* (Morellec et al., 2012, p. 803)". Management scholarship suggests that agency conflicts are heterogeneous across the stages of the life cycle of a firm, as the result of different free cash flow available, distinct growth perspectives, and of a different degree of alignment of interests between the managers, the shareholders, and the bondholders (Jensen, 1986; Filatotchev et al., 2006; Dickinson, 2011; O'Connor & Byrne, 2015a, 2015b). In this book, after having examined the literature investigating the relationship between taxes, agency conflicts, and the corporate capital structure, I attempt to answer the research question of whether tax avoidance activities are beneficial in reducing the debt covenant violation likelihood—a prominent real event affecting the capital structure—by empirically investigating the implications of such activities at each stage of the firm's life cycle. Specifically, drawing on the Agency Theory and on the corporate life cycle literature, I hypothesize that the effect of tax avoidance on the debt covenant violation likelihood is contingent to the life cycle stage the firm is in, as it can condition ex-ante the level of agency conflicts on the free cash flow and the related agency advantage expected from debt (Jensen, 1986; Vos & Forlong, 1996; Dickinson, 2011). The empirical evidence provided upon investigating a large sample of U.S public firms confirm such hypothesis.

The research findings show that, in corporate life cycle stages featured by a limited agency conflict between the shareholders and the managers on the free cash flow and by limited agency advantage of debt, like the introduction and decline stage, firms engaging higher level of tax avoidance benefit of a lower debt covenant violation likelihood. This result indicate that cash tax savings from tax avoidance may provide a substantial source of financing for constrained introductory and decline firms, likely to be used to service debt positions and enhancing firm's value and performance, reducing the firm's debt covenant violation likelihood. Conversely, in life cycle stages featured by a higher level of free cash flow available disputed between the managers and shareholders and by higher agency advantage of debt, like the mature stage, tax avoidance is associated to a higher likelihood of debt covenant violation. This result indicates that mature firms are unlikely to benefit from tax avoidance to reduce their violation likelihood, owing to potential uncertainty regarding future cash flow (i.e., risk of penalties), possible financial reporting opacity, reputational risks, and managerial discretion on the use of the resources retrieved from tax avoidance.

Overall, this book can add to prior tax literature in several ways. First, this study can add to the Agency Theory of tax avoidance, by suggesting the centrality of the free cash flow and related life cycle-contingent cash flow pattern in explaining the association between tax avoidance, the cost of the capital structure, and the related firm's risk of default. To the best of the authors' knowledge, there is limited use in prior literature of the Jensen's free cash flow hypothesis (Jensen, 1986, 1988) to examine the consequences of tax avoidance for the corporate capital structure. While the Agency Theory has been—for decades—the dominant framework in corporate tax avoidance studies, the Agency Theory-based free cash flow hypothesis has been substantially overlooked by previous literature (see e.g., Crocker & Slemrod, 2005; Desai & Dharmapala, 2006, 2009; Desai et al., 2007). This study can, thus, offer an original, theoretically grounded, reconciliation of two competing Agency Theory-based views (i.e., the "tunneling view" and the "value-enhancing" view) regarding the effect of tax avoidance for the corporate capital structure, as emerged from prior literature. Although the book primarily focuses on debt covenant violation as a real event affecting the capital structure management of many firms, much of the theoretical considerations developed can plausibly be extended to other capital structure contingencies such as, the cost-of-capital, the default likelihood, and the risk of financial distress.[1]

Second, the research adds to the empirical literature investigating the consequences of tax avoidance for the debt covenants. Prior literature predicted conflicting view on the association between tax avoidance and debt covenants (Kim et al., 2010; Hasan et al., 2014; Platikanova, 2017). According to Kim et al. (2010), banks are willing to impose fewer covenant restrictions to aggressive tax avoider firms as they are less likely to violate covenants' terms. Conversely, other studies suggest that tax avoider firms are more likely to incur covenant violations and are burdened, on average, by more stringent financial conditions (e.g., Hasan et al., 2014; Platikanova, 2017). This study complements this stream of research showing that the effect of tax avoidance on the debt covenant violation likelihood is contingent to the life cycle stage of a firm. Specifically, introductory and decline tax avoider firms are more likely to reduce their covenant violation likelihood when engaging higher level of tax avoidance. Conversely, for firms in the mature stage, tax avoidance is likely to increase the risk of violation, possibly due to a higher uncertainty on future cash

---

[1] In their recent review, Habib et al. (2020) point out that debt covenant violation is usually an early warning signal of corporate financial distress and that it is intimately tied with increases in the firm's cost-of-capital, default and bankruptcy likelihood.

flow, a higher financial reporting opacity, reputational risks, and managerial discretion associated to the use of corporate resources.

Third, this study can also provide useful insights to the stream of tax literature that builds on the debt-tax avoidance substitution hypothesis to examine the relationship between tax avoidance, the cost of capital, and the related risk of default (e.g., Lim, 2011b; Richardson et al., 2014). Prior literature argues that a higher level of tax avoidance is expected to be associated with a lower cost of capital and a lower risk of default because it lowers the amount of outstanding debt, due to the debt substitution effect. This study suggests that, due to the substitution effect, a higher level of tax avoidance can be expected to increase to increase the cost of capital, the likelihood of debt covenant violation, and the related risk of default, if the marginal agency benefits of debt outweigh the agency costs of debt. In this way, this study caution researchers to consider the potential reduction of the agency benefits of debt (as induced by the substitution effect), when interpreting the results of their research.

Finally, this research provides a review of main theories and empirical evidence on the effect of tax avoidance on the capital structure, and the related interacting effect exerted by agency conflicts. In this sense, the book can be of interests for both experienced and early-stage scholars interested in the topic, as well as for a wide plethora of professionals such as investors, analysts, lenders, and other market participants. In the amid of the actual Covid-19 health crisis, both scholarly tax and capital structure research have gained momentum both among practitioners and policymakers (e.g., Demmou et al., 2021; Altman, 2021; Becker et al., 2021; De Vito & Gómez, 2020; Baldwin & Weder di Mauro, 2020; Djankov & Zhang, 2021). Urged by the Covid-19 triggered economic downturn, policymakers have enacted several measures aimed at supporting the businesses' operating stability and avoiding financial disruptions (Baldwin & Weder di Mauro, 2020; De Vito & Gómez, 2020). These policies have encompassed a wide set of spending measures, spanning from deferral of tax payments to credit support and capital preservation programs (Casanova et al., 2021). In this way, a better understanding of the interaction between tax avoidance and the capital structure management, including its theoretical underpinnings, can also be of interest for policymakers and regulatory agencies engaged in prompting a sustainable economic recovery in the aftermath of the Covid-19 crisis.

The remainder of the book is organized as follows. Chapter 2 provides the theoretical background on the role of taxes in the theory of capital structure. Chapter 3 describes the role of agency conflicts in conditioning the effect of tax avoidance for a firm's capital structure and on the relevance of debt covenants within the corporate capital structure management. Chapter 4 introduces to the concept of corporate life cycle from an agency perspective and highlights its importance in conditioning the effect of corporate tax avoidance for the debt covenant violation likelihood and the related firm's financial default risk. Chapter 5 provides an empirical investigation of the effect of tax avoidance on debt covenant violation likelihood for each stage of the corporate life cycle, by testing the hypothesis formulated in Chap. 4. Finally, the monograph ends with Chap. 6 providing conclusion suggesting potential avenues of future research.

References

Alexander, R. M., Gross, A., Huston, G. R., & Richardson, V. J. (2017). Market response to fin 48 adoption: A debt covenant theory. In *Advances in taxation*. Emerald.

Altman, E. I. (2021). Covid-19 and the credit cycle: 2020 revisited and 2021 outlook. *Journal of Credit Risk, 17*(4).

Baldwin, R., & Weder di Mauro, B. (2020). *Mitigating the covid economic crisis: Act fast and do whatever it takes*. VoxEU.org. CEPR Press. Retrieved from https://voxeu.org/content/mitigating-covid-economic-crisis-act-fast-and-do-whatever-it-takes

Becker, B., Hege, U., & Mella-Barral, P. (2021). *Corporate debt burdens threaten economic recovery after COVID-19: Planning for debt restructuring should start now*. VoxEu.org. Retrieved from https://voxeu.org/article/corporate-debt-burdens-threaten-economic-recovery-after-covid-19

Casanova, C., Hardy, B., & Onen, M. (2021). Covid-19 policy measures to support bank lending. *BIS Quarterly Review*, 45–59.

Crocker, K. J., & Slemrod, J. (2005). Corporate tax evasion with agency costs. *Journal of Public Economics, 89*(9), 1593–1610.

De Vito, A., & Gómez, J.-P. (2020). Estimating the COVID-19 cash crunch: Global evidence and policy. *Journal of Accounting and Public Policy, 39*(2), 106741.

De Vito, A., & Jacob, M. (2021, November 27). The role of creditor protection in lending and tax avoidance. *Journal of Financial and Quantitative Analysis*. Retrieved from SSRN: https://ssrn.com/abstract=3727201 or https://doi.org/10.2139/ssrn.3727201.

DeAngelo, H., & Masulis, R. W. (1980). Leverage and Dividend Irrelevancy Under Corporate and Personal Taxation. *The Journal of Finance, 35*(2), 453–464.

Demerjian, P. R., & Owens, E. L. (2016). Measuring the probability of financial covenant violation in private debt contracts. *Journal of Accounting and Economics, 61*(2–3), 433–447.

Demmou, L., Calligaris, S., Franco, G., Dlugosch, D., Adalet McGowan, M., & Sakha, S. (2021). *Insolvency and debt overhang following the COVID-19 outbreak: Assessment of risks and policy responses*. OECD Economics Department Working Papers No 1651. OECD.

Desai, M. A., & Dharmapala, D. (2006). Corporate tax avoidance and high-powered incentives. *Journal of Financial Economics, 79*(1), 145–179.

Desai, M. A., & Dharmapala, D. (2009). Corporate tax avoidance and firm value. *Review of Economics and Statistics, 91*(3), 537–546.

Desai, M. A., Dyck, A., & Zingales, L. (2007). Theft and taxes. *Journal of Financial Economics, 84*, 591–623.

Dhawan, A., Ma, L., & Kim, M. H. (2020). Effect of corporate tax avoidance activities on firm bankruptcy risk. *Journal of Contemporary Accounting and Economics, 16*(2), 100187.

Dichev, I. D., & Skinner, D. J. (2002). Large–sample evidence on the debt covenant hypothesis. *Journal of Accounting Research, 40*(4), 1091–1123.

Dickinson, V. (2011). Cash flow patterns as a proxy for firm life cycle. *The Accounting Review, 86*(6), 1969–1994.

Djankov, S., & Zhang, E. (2021). *As COVID rages, bankruptcy cases fall*. VoxEu.org. Retrieved from https://voxeu.org/article/covid-rages-bankruptcy-cases-fall

Dyreng, S. D., Hillegeist, S. A., & Penalva, F. (2022). Earnings management to avoid debt covenant violations and future performance. *European Accounting Review, 31*(2), 311–343.

Edwards, A., Schwab, C., & Shevlin, T. (2016). Financial constraints and cash tax savings. *The Accounting Review, 91*(3), 859–881.

Eisenhardt, K. M. (1989). Agency theory: An assessment and review. *The Academy of Management Review, 14*(1), 57–74.

Filatotchev, I., Toms, S., & Wright, M. (2006). The firm's strategic dynamics and corporate governance life-cycle. *International Journal of Managerial Finance, 2*(4), 256–279.

Freudenberg, F., Imbierowicz, B., Saunders, A., & Steffen, S. (2017). Covenant violations and dynamic loan contracting. *Journal of Corporate Finance, 45*, 540–565.

Gao, Y., Khan, M., & Tan, L. (2017). Further evidence on consequences of debt covenant violations. *Contemporary Accounting Research, 34*(3), 1489–1521.

Graham, J. R., & Tucker, A. L. (2006). Tax shelters and corporate debt policy. *Journal of Financial Economics, 81*, 563–594.

Guenther, D. A., Njoroge, K., & Williams, B. M. (2020). Allocation of internal cash flow when firms pay less tax. *The Accounting Review, 95*(5), 185–210.

Habib, A., Costa, M. D., Huang, H. J., Bhuiyan, M. B. U., & Sun, L. (2020). Determinants and consequences of financial distress: Review of the empirical literature. *Accounting and Finance, 60*, 1023–1075.

Hasan, I., Hoi, C. K. S., Wu, Q., & Zhang, H. (2014). Beauty is in the eye of the beholder: The effect of corporate tax avoidance on the cost of bank loans. *Journal of Financial Economics, 113*(1), 109–130.

Jensen, M. C. (1986). Agency costs of free cash flow, corporate finance, and takeovers. *The American Economic Review, 76*, 323–329. https://doi.org/10.2139/ssrn.99580

Jensen, M. C. (1988). Takeovers: Their causes and consequences. *Journal of Economic Perspectives, 2*(1), 21–48.

Jensen, M. C., & Meckling, W. H. (1976). Theory of the firm: Managerial behavior, agency costs and ownership structure. *Journal of Financial Economics, 3*(4), 305–360.

Kim, J. B., Li, O. Z., & Li, Y. (2010). *Corporate tax avoidance and bank loan contracting.* Available at SSRN 1596209.

Lee, Y., Shevlin, T., & Venkat, A. (2022). The effect of tax avoidance on capital structure choices. *Journal of the American Taxation Association.* https://doi.org/10.2308/JATA-19-049

Lim, Y. (2011a). Tax avoidance and underleverage puzzle: Korean evidence. *Review of Quantitative Finance and Accounting, 39*(3), 333–360.

Lim, Y. (2011b). Tax avoidance, cost of debt and shareholder activism: Evidence from Korea. *Journal of Banking and Finance, 35*(2), 456–470.

Lin, S., Tong, N., & Tucker, A. L. (2014). Corporate tax aggression and debt. *Journal of Banking and Finance, 40*, 227–241.

MacKie-Mason, J. K. (1990). Do taxes affect corporate financing decisions? *Journal of Finance, 45*, 1471–1493.

Morellec, E., Nikolov, B., & Schürhoff, N. (2012). Corporate governance and capital structure dynamics. *The Journal of Finance, 67*(3), 803–848.

Myers, S. C. (1977). Determinants of corporate borrowing. *Journal of Financial Economics, 5*(2), 147–175.

O'Connor, T., & Byrne, J. (2015a). Governance and the corporate life-cycle. *International Journal of Managerial Finance, 11*(1), 23–43.

O'Connor, T., & Byrne, J. (2015b). When does corporate governance matter? Evidence from across the corporate life-cycle. *Managerial Finance, 41*(7), 673–691.

Platikanova, P. (2017). Debt maturity and tax avoidance. *European Accounting Review, 26*(1), 97–124.

Richardson, G., Lanis, R., & Leung, S. C. M. (2014). Corporate tax aggressiveness, outside directors, and debt policy: An empirical analysis. *Journal of Corporate Finance, 25*, 107–121.

Roberts, M. R., & Sufi, A. (2009). Renegotiation of financial contracts: Evidence from private credit agreements. *Journal of Financial Economics, 93*(2), 159–184.

Smith, C. W., Jr., & Warner, J. B. (1979). On financial contracting: An analysis of bond covenants. *Journal of Financial Economics, 7*(2), 117–161.

Vos, E., & Forlong, C. (1996). The agency advantage of debt over the lifecycle of the firm. *The Journal of Entrepreneurial Finance, 5*(3), 193–211.

Chapter 2
Tax Avoidance as a Source of Financing

Keywords Tax avoidance · Financing decisions · Capital structure · Cost-of-capital

2.1 The Role of Taxes in the Theory of Capital Structure

In a first attempt to investigate firms' financial policies and related capital structure decisions, Modigliani and Miller (1958) developed a framework based on assumptions that are rarely to find in the real business world (i.e., no taxes; no agency costs; no bankruptcy costs; perfect information). In a later article, published in 1963, however, Modigliani and Miller recognized that tax interest deductibility may incentive firms to use debt (Modigliani & Miller, 1963; Graham, 2003; see also: Hanlon and Heitzman (2010) for a review). From this point onward, taxation (both at a personal and corporate level) assumed a crucial role in the subsequent corporate finance research (e.g., Miller, 1977; DeAngelo & Masulis, 1980; Myers, 1984). Relaxing the initial assumptions of the Modigliani-Miller model, later theoretical models added further insights on the tradeoff between tax benefits (i.e., debt interest deductibility) and non-tax costs, such as the consideration of agency costs and bankruptcy costs (Jensen & Meckling, 1976; Myers, 1977; Leland, 1998). Consistent with the idea that any tax advantage should be compared against with any potential non-tax costs, Scholes et al. (1992) argue that a firm's tax planning decision should carefully consider "all taxes", "all parties", and "all costs" (i.e., non-tax costs) embedded in a business transaction.

To date, the main theoretical frameworks developed to describe firms' capital structure choices are, among the others: (1) the *"Trade-off Theory"* (Kraus & Litzenberger, 1973), which suggests that the firm's optimal capital structure is achieved by balancing tax benefits of debt with the bankruptcy costs associated with debt financing; (2) the *"Agency Theory"* (e.g., Jensen & Meckling, 1976; Lasfer, 1995; Ashbaugh-Skaife et al., 2006), that posits the conflict between shareholders (i.e., *principal*) and managers (i.e., *agents*) (Jensen & Meckling, 1976; Fama & Jensen, 1983), and that one between shareholders and bondholders (Jensen, 1986, 1988) as a primary condition in determining firms' financing decisions (Lasfer, 1995); (3) the *"Signaling Theory"* (Ross, 1977), which suggests that capital market participants perceive debt issues (rather than equity issues) as a signal of corporate performance; (4) the *"Pecking Order Theory"* (Myers, 1984; Myers & Majluf, 1984), which posits that, due to information asymmetries, firms prefer internal (e.g., retained earnings) versus external source of financing (with debt preferred over equity). While these theories provide distinctive frameworks for the analysis of the corporate capital structure, these theories are not necessarily to be considered as mutually exclusive (Graham, 2003). Rather, the same capital structure phenomena could be interpreted by considering one or more of these theories.

Most of the capital structure theories indicated acknowledge corporate taxes as fundamental aspect to consider when making financing decisions. Although the emphasis on taxation can vary depending on the theory considered, collectively these theories suggest that tax choices can have a primary role in determining the design and the cost of firms' capital structure. Therefore, tax avoidance—i.e., the firm's decision to minimize tax expenditures[1]—can be considered as a complementary part of firm's capital structure management and, as such, be interpreted on a par with other firm's incremental capital structure decisions (i.e., debt vs. equity decisions) (Richardson et al., 2015, p. 44; see also: Noga & Schnader, 2013; Lin et al., 2014; Bayar et al., 2018; Dhawan et al., 2020).

2.2   The Debt-Tax Avoidance Substitution Hypothesis

Tax scholars suggest that tax avoidance may be viewed as an alternative source of financing through which to potentially replace other, more expensive, source of funds (e.g., Guenther et al., 2020; Edwards et al., 2016; Richardson et al., 2015). This view lies its theoretical foundations on the DeAngelo and Masulis (1980) *"debt substitution hypothesis"* (also referred to as *"debt-tax avoidance substitution"*), which suggests that non-debt tax shields (e.g., tax avoidance/sheltering) may substitute for the tax advantages of debt.[2] In their seminal contribution, DeAngelo and Masulis (1980) show that an increase in the firm's depreciation deductions—a form of non-debt tax shield—is positively associated with a decline in the firm's demand for debt interests' deductions. Following studies have tested this hypothesis and have found some supporting evidence, particularly for firms facing financial constraints (e.g., MacKie-Mason, 1990; Trezevant, 1992, p. 1157; Graham, 2000; Graham

---

[1] Consistently with prior studies, this review defines tax avoidance (planning) as "a broad range of tax payment reduction activities, spanning from legal tax strategies compliant with tax law (e.g., benign tax-advantaged investments) to more aggressive strategies with a higher likelihood of being disallowed upon audit by tax authorities (e.g., aggressive interpretation of ambiguous areas of tax law)" (Hanlon & Heitzman, 2010; Akamah et al., 2021).

[2] Following prior studies, this paper uses the terms non-debt tax shield and tax avoidance as interchangeable (Lim, 2011a, 2011b; Lin et al., 2014; De Vito & Jacob, 2021). Hence, the term non-debt tax shields is used to include both benign tax advantages compliant with the law (e.g., depreciation, depletion allowances, investment tax credits, and deferred tax losses) and aggressive tax strategies (e.g., tax shelters) (see: De Vito & Jacob, 2021, p. 1).

et al., 2004; Graham & Tucker, 2006; Wilson, 2009; Lim, 2011a, 2011b; Lin et al., 2014; Edwards et al., 2016; Lanis et al., 2021; De Vito & Jacob, 2021).

MacKie-Mason (1990) examines the effect of taxes on the choice between debt for equity and provides evidence of the impact of non-debt tax shields (i.e., tax losses carryforwards and investment tax credits) on the firm's debt policy and related incremental capital structure decisions. In his study, MacKie-Mason (1990) finds that non-debt tax shields are a substitute of debt-tax shields and that such substitutive relation is more pronounced in firms more likely to lose their debt tax shields deductibility. This effect has been referred to as tax exhaustion effect (Trezevant, 1992, p. 1557).

To further provide evidence on the existence of a substitution effect between the two classes of tax shields, Trezevant (1992) exploits, in his study, the unique setting offered by the enactment of the 1981 Economic Recovery Tax Act. By controlling for the debt securitability,[3] Trezevant (1992) finds that the level of debt is negatively associated with the level of non-debt tax shields and that, in line with the tax exhaustion hypothesis, the substitutive relation observed is stronger for firms with a higher probability of losing the deductibility of such tax shields.

A similar insight at support of the substitution effect is also provided by Graham (2000). Examining how large are the tax benefits associated with debt financing, Graham (2000) shows that, on average, firms pursue conservative leverage strategies compared with the possible tax advantage associated to the leverage financing. According to the author, this effect is particularly strong in firms that are "*large, liquid, and profitable*" and in those with low expected bankruptcy costs. Although this finding was described by the author as apparently "*paradoxical*", this finding might not be surprising if the presence of non-debt tax sheltering is taken into account (Graham, 2000).

Four years later, Graham et al. (2004) examined the aggregate level of tax savings resulting from employee stock options deductions of a sample of Nasdaq 100 and S&P 100 firms. The authors find that option deductions constitute a relevant non-debt tax shield for many businesses included in the sample and that this form of tax shield partially contribute to explain the conservative debt policies undertaken by the firms examined. Importantly, the authors' argument, here, is not that firms engage in tax shelters to reduce their level of debt but, rather, that firms engage in tax sheltering to minimize their income tax expenditures: as long as tax shelters are effective in reducing the firm's taxable income, firms will be less likely to use debt as a source of financing (Graham & Tucker, 2006, p. 569).

To furtherly parse out the association between debt and non-debt tax shields, Graham and Tucker (2006) investigate a sample of 43 public firms, from 1975 to 2000, alleged for having engaged in illegal tax shelters. Results of the analyses indicate that tax shelters significantly affect the firms' debt policy. Specifically, the

---

[3] Debt securitability refers to the possibility for lenders to use fixed assets as collateral. Thus, an increase in investment in fixed assets (to be used as collateral for debt) might offset the substitution effect.

authors find that the debt-to-asset ratios of firms engaging in tax sheltering are on average lower than 5% compared to those of firms not engaging in tax sheltering. Findings from Graham and Tucker (2006) constitute another significant evidence at support of the existence of a substitutive association between the two types of tax shields and contribute to deeply understand the association already observed in Graham et al. (2004).

Despite this evidence, however, Graham and Tucker (2006) results are not without limitations. Specifically, the limited number of firms investigated has raised concerns of lack of generalizability of their results (Graham & Tucker, 2006, p. 566). This limitation is well-known in the literature (e.g., Lim, 2011a, 2011b; De Vito & Jacob, 2021). Nonetheless, the literature also acknowledges that the use of small sample size is a common limitation of most the research on tax shelters, given the difficulty to detect *ex-ante* the firm's sheltering participation (Wilson, 2009).

To overcome this limitation, Wilson (2009) elaborates a score which allows to predict the likelihood that a firm is engaging in a tax shelter. By investigating a sample of 59 firms accused by the government of participating in tax shelters,[4] Wilson collects a set of common accounting and governance characteristics of sheltering firms. Using these characteristics, he elaborates a logistic model that predicts the firm's likelihood to be engaged in a tax shelter. The model proposed by Wilson is defined as: Ln $(Pshelter/1 - Pshelter) = \beta\chi + \varepsilon_t$. Where, Ln $(Pshelter/1 - Pshelter)$ represents the probability that the firm examined is engaging in a tax shelter, while χ is a matrix containing the following variables: book-tax differences (BTDs); a measure of discretionary accruals (DAP); leverage (LEV); size (SIZE); return on total assets (ROA); existence of foreign income (FOREIGN INCOME); level of research and development scaled for total assets (R&D).[5]

Later studies have used the Wilson's score model to broaden the set of empirical evidence on the relationship between tax avoidance and capital structure (e.g., Lin et al., 2014). For example, using a sample of U.S. public firms, Lin et al. (2014) add to previous studies by showing that, although debt is inversely associated with corporate tax aggressiveness in most of the firms included in the sample—particularly for firms with higher tax-shelter prediction scores—there is no evidence of substitution in highly profitable firms. A similar result is also provided by a concurrent paper, which shows that the substitution effect is dissipated when examining very large, high profitable firms, and firms with high credit rating (Rao & Yu, 2013).

In the last years, additional insights on the debt-tax avoidance substitution effect have also emerged from investigation of samples of non-US firms. For example, Lim (2011b) investigates a sample of Korean firms; Lanis et al. (2021) examine a sample

---

[4]Tax shelters considered by Wilson (2009) are: (a) the Lease-In, Lease-Out (LILO); Corporate-Owned Life Insurance; Contest Liability Acceleration Strategy (CLAS); Contingent-Payment Installment Sales (CPIS); Cross-Border Dividend Capture (CBDC); Transfer Pricing; Offshore Intellectual Property (OIPH); 401(k) Deduction Acceleration Strategy; Interest rate swaps; money market principal strips; sham transactions.

[5]Lisowsky (2010) extended the framework elaborated by Wilson (2009) by adding more firm characteristics and testing the prediction model on a wider sample of firms.

of Australian firms, while De Vito and Jacob (2021) a sample of Italian and European firms. Overall, these studies confirm the hypothesis of substitution between debt and tax avoidance.[6] However, compared to previous research, these studies added to this line of literature in many new important ways.

The research of Lim (2011b) starts by replicating Graham and Tucker (2006) in a sample of Korean firms but adding the impact of tax avoidance on the cost of debt as additional examination. Overall, his results are in line with prior literature and confirm the existence of a negative association between debt (and its cost) and tax avoidance. In a similar vein, Richardson et al. (2014) also provide evidence of a negative association between tax avoidance and debt. However, differently from previous studies, Richardson et al. (2014) also find that the examined association is stronger when the impact of outside directors is considered. Therefore, the authors conclude that, while a debt-tax avoidance substitution effect exists, corporate governance characteristics can have an important effect in modulating the intensity of such substitution and, as such, their consideration can contribute to a better understanding on how firms use tax avoidance as a source of funds alternative to debt financing. Starting from these insights, and investigating a sample of Australian public firms, Lanis et al. (2021) show that the board of directors impacts on the debt-tax avoidance substitution. Specifically, their results suggest that the substitution effect is stronger when there are outside directors with financial expertise in the board of directors.

Besides corporate governance characteristics, specific country-level institutional features are also likely to affect the debt-tax avoidance relationship. In a recent research, De Vito and Jacob (2021) contribute to this literature by arguing that the legal environment in which the firm operates is an aspect to carefully consider when examining such tradeoff. Focusing on the creditor rights protection, the authors show that strong creditors' rights are associated with an increase of debt financing (i.e., bank lending) and a significant reduction of tax avoidance activities.

2.3 Implications of Tax Avoidance for the Capital Structure

Overall, most of the literature, so far, has provided evidence consistent with DeAngelo and Masulis (1980) prediction. While the empirical evidence on the "debt substitution hypothesis" is far from being conclusive, most of the studies examined converge in showing that firms with higher level of tax avoidance have, on

---

[6]Besides the investigation of specific country settings, other studies have examined the effect of tax policies (both at a personal and corporate level). In this vein, Rajan and Zingales (1995) examined the combined effect of personal and corporate taxes on the capital structure using G-7 countries' tax reforms. Faccio and Xu (2015) used a comprehensive sample of OECD 561 country-year observations from 1981 to 2009 and testing 184 changes in corporate tax rates and 289 changes in personal tax rates, respectively.

average, a lower level of indebtment.[7] Taking a different perspective, this result could suggest an impact of tax avoidance on equity financing decisions as well. Indeed, despite a paucity of empirical evidence on the association between tax avoidance and equity financing decisions, some studies have shown that tax aggressive firms and firms with high level of non-debt tax shields are more likely to choose to issue more equity and less debt (e.g., Lee et al., 2022).

An extension of the debt substitution hypothesis might also suggest that, given the relationship of tax avoidance with the other source of financing, the level of tax avoidance could affect not only the composition of the firm's capital structure, but also is cost (e.g., Lim, 2011b; Lin et al., 2014).

Finance research shows that leverage financing increases the firms' expected bankruptcy costs and the related cost of debt (Baxter, 1967; Brennan & Schwartz, 1978; Chen, 1978). This relation is well exposed by Leland (1994): "*As leverage increases, the tax advantage of debt eventually will be offset by increased cost of debt, reflecting the greater likelihood of financial distress*" (Leland, 1994, p. 1213). Therefore, it can be argued that, by switching debt for tax avoidance, firms might improve their financial health. On the one hand, firms engaging higher level of tax avoidance can benefit of a higher credit quality, a reduced cost of debt, a lower debt covenant violation likelihood, and a lower risk of bankruptcy (Kim et al., 2010; Lim, 2011b; Bayar et al., 2018). On the other, they can also take advantage of a lower cost of equity capital, since tax avoidance increases the level of the cash flow that is expected by the shareholders (Goh et al., 2016).[8]

However, it has to be noted that the aforesaid consideration, based on the studies examined, does not directly consider the impact of stakeholders' conflicting interests on the resources retrieved from corporate tax avoidance activities, which can eventually offset or reverse the expected effect. In this respect, Hasan et al. (2014) argue that corporate stakeholders have different incentive and different expectations regarding firms' tax avoidance activities. For example, bondholders and other fixed claimants would perceive tax avoidance negatively, since they bear the risks related to such activities without modifying their expectation about future returns. Similarly, equity-holders, although potentially beneficiaries of tax avoidance activities, could perceive tax avoidance as a signal of risk and increased agency conflicts, thus increasing the cost of equity capital required (Kim et al., 2011). As a result, the expected effect of tax avoidance on a firm's capital structure could change if agency conflicts pertaining to tax avoidance and capital structure decisions are considered. In the following chapter, I provide an outline of the agency theory and a synthesis of the literature that examines the effects of tax avoidance on a firm's capital structure,

---

[7]There are some studies that failed in finding an inverse relation between debt and tax avoidance. However, a potential limitation of these research is given by the fact that the non-debt tax shields can also proxy for profitability, which is usually positively related to the leverage (MacKie-Mason, 1990; see Graham (1996) proxies for the corporate marginal tax rate).

[8]Specifically, Goh et al. (2016) suggest that, although tax avoidance could increase the risks for shareholders, such effect can be offset and outweighed by an additive effect of tax avoidance on the level of cash flow that is expected by shareholders, thus reducing the cost of equity.

once agency conflicts between the managers, the shareholders, and the bondholders are taken into account.

References

Akamah, H. T., Omer, T. C., & Shu, S. Q. (2021). Financial constraints and future tax outcome volatility. *Journal of Business Finance and Accounting, 48*(3–4), 637–665.

Ashbaugh-Skaife, H., Collins, D. W., & LaFond, R. (2006). The effects of corporate governance on firms' credit ratings. *Journal of Accounting and Economics, 42*(1–2), 203–243.

Baxter, N. (1967). Leverage, risk of ruin and the cost of capital. *Journal of Finance, 3*, 395–403.

Bayar, O., Huseynov, F., & Sardarli, S. (2018). Corporate governance, Tax avoidance, and financial constraints. *Financial Management, 47*(3), 651–677.

Brennan, M. J., & Schwartz, E. S. (1978). Corporate income taxes, valuation, and the problem of optimal capital structure. *Journal of Business, 51*, 103–114.

Chen, A. H. (1978). Recent developments in the cost of debt capital. *The Journal of Finance, 33*(3), 863–877.

De Vito, A., & Jacob, M. (2021, November 27). *The role of creditor protection in lending and tax avoidance.* Available at SSRN: https://ssrn.com/abstract=3727201 or https://doi.org/10.2139/ssrn.3727201

DeAngelo, H., & Masulis, R. W. (1980). Leverage and dividend irrelevancy under corporate and personal taxation. *The Journal of Finance, 35*(2), 453–464.

Dhawan, A., Ma, L., & Kim, M. H. (2020). Effect of corporate tax avoidance activities on firm bankruptcy risk. *Journal of Contemporary Accounting & Economics, 16*(2), 100187.

Edwards, A., Schwab, C., & Shevlin, T. (2016). Financial constraints and cash tax savings. *The Accounting Review, 91*(3), 859–881.

Faccio, M., & Xu, J. (2015). Taxes and capital structure. *Journal of Financial and Quantitative Analysis, 50*(3), 277–300.

Fama, E. F., & Jensen, M. C. (1983). Separation of ownership and control. *The Journal of Law and Economics, 26*(2), 301–325.

Goh, B. W., Lee, J., Lim, C. Y., & Shevlin, T. (2016). The effect of corporate tax avoidance on the cost of equity. *The Accounting Review, 91*(6), 1647–1670.

Graham, J. R. (1996). Debt and the marginal tax rate. *Journal of Financial Economics, 41*(1), 41–73.

Graham, J. R. (2000). How big are the tax benefits of debt? *Journal of Finance, 55*, 1901–1942.

Graham, J. R. (2003). Taxes and corporate finance: A review. *The Review of Financial Studies, 16*(4), 1075–1129.

Graham, J. R., Lang, M. H., & Shackelford, D. A. (2004). Employee stock options, corporate taxes, and debt policy. *The Journal of Finance, 59*(4), 1585–1618.

Graham, J. R., & Tucker, A. L. (2006). Tax shelters and corporate debt policy. *Journal of Financial Economics, 81*, 563–594.

Guenther, D. A., Njoroge, K., & Williams, B. M. (2020). Allocation of internal cash flow when firms pay less tax. *The Accounting Review, 95*(5), 185–210.

Hanlon, M., & Heitzman, S. (2010). A review of tax research. *Journal of Accounting and Economics, 50*(2–3), 127–178.

Hasan, I., Hoi, C. K. S., Wu, Q., & Zhang, H. (2014). Beauty is in the eye of the beholder: The effect of corporate tax avoidance on the cost of bank loans. *Journal of Financial Economics, 113*(1), 109–130.

Jensen, M. C. (1986). Agency costs of free cash flow, corporate finance, and takeovers. *The American Economic Review, 76*, 323–329. https://doi.org/10.2139/ssrn.99580

Jensen, M. C. (1988). Takeovers: Their causes and consequences. *Journal of Economic Perspectives, 2*(1), 21–48.

Jensen, M. C., & Meckling, W. H. (1976). Theory of the firm: Managerial behavior, agency costs and ownership structure. *Journal of Financial Economics, 3*(4), 305–360.

Kim, J. B., Li, O. Z., & Li, Y. (2010). Corporate tax avoidance and bank loan contracting. *Working paper.*. Available at SSRN 1596209.

Kim, J. B., Li, Y., & Zhang, L. (2011). Corporate tax avoidance and stock price crash risk: Firm-level analysis. *Journal of Financial Economics, 100*(3), 639–662.

Kraus, A., & Litzenberger, R. H. (1973). A state-preference model of optimal financial leverage. *The Journal of Finance, 28*(4), 911–922.

Lanis, R., Richardson, G., Govendir, B., & Pazmandy, G. (2021). The effect of board of directors' expertise and tax avoidance on corporate debt. *Accounting and Finance, 61*(3), 4475–4511.

Lasfer, M. A. (1995). Agency costs, taxes and debt: The UK evidence. *European Financial Management, 1*(3), 265–285.

Lee, Y., Shevlin, T. J., & Venkat, A. (2022). The effect of tax avoidance on capital structure choices. *Journal of American Taxation Association.* https://doi.org/10.2308/JATA-19-049

Leland, H. E. (1994). Corporate debt value, bond covenants, and optimal capital structure. *The Journal of Finance, 49*(4), 1213–1252.

Leland, H. E. (1998). Agency costs, risk management, and capital structure. *The Journal of Finance, 53*(4), 1213–1243.

Lim, Y. (2011a). Tax avoidance and underleverage puzzle: Korean evidence. *Review of Quantitative Finance and Accounting, 39*(3), 333–360.

Lim, Y. (2011b). Tax avoidance, cost of debt and shareholder activism: Evidence from Korea. *Journal of Banking and Finance, 35*(2), 456–470.

Lin, S., Tong, N., & Tucker, A. L. (2014). Corporate tax aggression and debt. *Journal of Banking and Finance, 40*, 227–241.

Lisowsky, P. (2010). Seeking shelter: Empirically modeling tax shelters using financial statement information. *The Accounting Review, 85*(5), 1693–1720.

MacKie-Mason, J. K. (1990). Do taxes affect corporate financing decisions? *Journal of Finance, 45*, 1471–1493.

Miller, M. H. (1977). Debt and taxes. *The Journal of Finance, 32*(2), 261–275.

Modigliani, F., & Miller, M. H. (1958). The cost of capital, corporation finance and the theory of investment. *The American Economic Review, 48*, 261–297.

Modigliani, F., & Miller, M. H. (1963). Corporate income taxes and the cost of capital: A correction. *American Economic Review, 53*, 433–443.

Myers, S. C. (1977). Determinants of corporate borrowing. *Journal of Financial Economics, 5*(2), 147–175.

Myers, S. C. (1984). *Capital structure puzzle.* NBER Working Paper (w1393).

Myers, S. C., & Majluf, N. S. (1984). Corporate financing and investment decisions when firms have information that investors do not have. *Journal of Financial Economics, 13*(2), 187–221.

Noga, T. J., & Schnader, A. L. (2013). Book-tax differences as an indicator of financial distress. *Accounting Horizons, 27*(3), 469–489.

Rajan, R. G., & Zingales, L. (1995). What do we know about capital structure? Some evidence from international data. *The Journal of Finance, 50*(5), 1421–1460.

Rao, R. P., & Yu, T. R. (2013). *Corporate tax avoidance and debt policy.* Available at SSRN 2352646.

Richardson, G., Lanis, R., & Leung, S. C. M. (2014). Corporate tax aggressiveness, outside directors, and debt policy: An empirical analysis. *Journal of Corporate Finance, 25*, 107–121.

Richardson, G., Taylor, G., & Lanis, R. (2015). The impact of financial distress on corporate tax avoidance spanning the global financial crisis: Evidence from Australia. *Economic Modelling, 44*, 44–53.

Ross, S. A. (1977). The determination of financial structure: The incentive-signalling approach. *The Bell Journal of Economics, 8*, 23–40.

Scholes, M. S., Wolfson, M. A., Erickson, M., Maydew, E., & Shevlin, T. (1992). *Taxes and business strategy: A planning approach.* Prentice-Hall.

Trezevant, R. (1992). Debt financing and tax status: Tests of the substitution effect and the tax exhaustion hypothesis using firms' responses to the Economic Recovery Tax Act of 1981. *Journal of Finance, 47*, 1557–1568.

Wilson, R. J. (2009). An examination of corporate tax shelter participants. *The Accounting Review, 84*(3), 969–999.

Chapter 3
Tax Avoidance and Capital Structure in an Agency Perspective

Keywords Tax avoidance · Agency conflicts · Free cash flow · Cost-of-capital · Financial default · Debt covenants

3.1 Agency Theory: An Overview

The Agency theory, as formalized by Jensen and Meckling (1976), stems, on the one hand, from the theory of property rights (Coase, 1937; Alchian & Demsetz, 1972), which interprets the firm as a "*nexus of contracts*" among independent parties and, on the other hand, from the risk-sharing literature, which examines the relations of cooperation among individuals having different risk appetites (Wilson, 1968; Arrow, 1971).

Besides the theory of property rights and the risk-sharing literature, the Agency Theory has also received, directly or indirectly, important conceptual underpinnings from other works, including, but not limited to: the Classical economics (e.g., Smith, 1776); the early 30s researches on the large U.S. public corporations' ownership and control (Bearle & Means, 1932); the Bureaucratic theory of Max Weber and its concurrent critique (Weber, 1947; Merton, 1940), the theory of Herbert Simon on bounded rationality and information asymmetries (Simon, 1965). Other relevant theoretical inputs to the development of the Agency theory are also to be found in Barnard's "theory of opportunism" and "power of choice" (Barnard, 1938) and in the Mary Parker Follett's studies on conflicts and cooperative resolutions (Follett, 1924).[1]

As any theory, even the Agency theory has several limitations and relies on a specific set of assumptions (Shleifer & Vishny, 1997; Daily et al., 2003). A fundamental assumption of the Agency theory is the existence of a contractual agreement between two or more parties for a non-better identified future time (Panda & Leepsa, 2017). Additionally, in the agency framework, individuals are described as boundedly rational, risk-adverse, and self-interest motivated economic actors,

---

[1] For a detailed historical review of the groundworks of the Agency theory, here briefly reported (see: Bendickson et al., 2016; Panda & Leepsa, 2017, pp. 77–79).

endowed of a limited set of information that is typically asymmetric to the information held by the other contracting part (Eisenhardt, 1989).

Starting from its early developments, the Agency Theory has been subject to an intense debate among scholars (e.g., Kaplan & Ruland, 1991). On the one hand, the supporters of the Agency Theory emphasized the universal and comprehensive character of the framework (Jensen & Roeback, 1983). On the other, opponents argued that, given its conjectures, the Agency theory was too simplistic, a-moral, and even *"dangerous"* (Perrow, 1986; see: Eisenhardt, 1989, p. 57; Roberts, 2005, p. 253).

Despite such debate, however, the Agency Theory has represented and continues to represent an important, if not the *most* important, theoretical framework in the fields of positivist accounting and financial economics, with considerable influence in many other disciplines outside the field of economics (Watts & Zimmerman, 1986; Eisenhardt, 1989; Wagenhofer, 2015).

3.1.1   The Shareholders-Managers Conflict

In its basic formulation, the Agency Theory suggests that agency relationships might arise all the time in which one or more parties, known as *principal*, engage with one or more other parties, known as *agent*, to perform some actions on their behalf (Ross, 1973; Jensen & Meckling, 1976; Hill & Jones, 1992, p. 132). According to the theory, both the principal and the agent are economic actors willing to maximize their personal utility functions (Jensen & Meckling, 1976). Ideally, the agent's best interest should coincide with the principal's best interest. More often, however, the interests of the agent are not aligned with the interests of the principal. Therefore, the relation between the two parties may be subject to agency conflicts.

Agency conflicts arise all the time in which two or more cooperating parties have different goals and a different set of information (Jensen & Meckling, 1976; Eisenhardt, 1989). Since the principal starts the relationship with the agent by delegating a certain decision-making authority, the principal will have a limited knowledge on the activities undertaken by the agent. As a result, the agent can use its informative advantage to carry-out activities aimed at maximizing their personal utility at the expenses of the principal.

In a business context, the archetypal agency conflict is represented by the relationship between shareholders (i.e., principal) and managers (i.e., agent). Since shareholders delegate managers to accomplish business activities, shareholders usually have limited knowledge on the costs and revenues sources pertaining to the business. Therefore, in the absence of appropriate means to control managerial actions, managers could use their informative advantage to maximize their personal wealth (Jensen & Meckling, 1976; Fama & Jensen, 1983; Watts & Zimmerman, 1986).

Agency conflicts between shareholders and managers are at the bases of any firm. Hence, any relationship between these two parties will always entail certain costs.

These costs, also known as "*agency costs*", are borne by both the contracting parties and can take different forms.

A first source of agency costs is represented by all the expenditures sustained by the shareholders (i.e., principal) to set up mechanisms aimed at monitoring the actions undertaken by the agent. These costs are referred as *monitoring costs*. A typical example of monitoring cost is represented by the expenditure requested for arranging periodical external and internal audits.

In addition to the monitoring costs, the principal can also incur in certain form of *bonding costs*. Bonding costs encompass all the expenditures that the principal sustain in order to limit the opportunistic behavior of the agents and to guarantee that the actions of the agents is not harmful for them. A typical example of bonding cost is represented by the cost to set up a scheme of incentives and compensation aimed at stimulating managerial actions aligned with the principal's best interest.

Both the monitoring and bonding costs are borne by the principal. However, the principal is not the only one anguished by agency costs. Agency costs can be borne by the agent as well. Costs borne by the agent are typically in the form of *ex-ante* bonding costs, which can be defined as "*a mix of monetary or non-monetary expenditures sustained by the agents and necessary to acquire the right of managing the principal's resources*" (see: Hill & Jones, 1992, p. 132).

Empirical investigation of the Agency Theory suggests that the conflict between shareholders (i.e., the principal) and managers (i.e., the agents) is a fundamental aspect to consider when examining firms' real decisions, including incremental financing decisions and capital structure choices (e.g., Maksimovic & Zechner, 1991; Lasfer, 1995). However, it is important to note that the agency relationship between managers and shareholders constitutes only a part of the complex nexus of relations taking place in a firm. Consistently, agency theorists have suggested to broaden the plethora of subjects to be included into the agency examination. In this respect, Jensen (1986) extended the traditional agency conflicts between shareholders and managers to the bondholders, whilst Hill and Jones (1992) proposed an articulated framework in which the corporate principal-agent relation is interpreted as the agency conflicts between the stakeholders (i.e., shareholders, managers, creditors, employees, suppliers, communities and the general public) and managers.

3.1.2 The Shareholders-Bondholders Conflict and the Agency Benefits of Debt

In 1986, Jensen formulated a variant of the traditional Agency theory that integrates the central role played by the firm's free cash flow (i.e., the "*free cash flow hypothesis*") and the agency conflicts between shareholders and bondholders into the previous framework centered on the managers-shareholders relationship (Jensen & Meckling, 1976). Particularly, the main intuition of Jensen (1986) is that of considering the agency conflicts between shareholders and bondholders as a crucial aspect in shaping the severity of the agency conflicts between managers and share-holders on the use and allocation of the free cash flow and, as such, in determining the consequent capital structure decisions made by the firm.

Jensen (1986, 1988) define the free cash flow as the *"cash flow in excess of that required to fund all projects that have positive net present values when discounted at a relevant cost of capital"* (see: Jensen, 1986, p. 323; Jensen, 1988, p. 28). Therefore, basing on this definition, the free cash flow is the cash flow pertaining to the firm that remains once all the profitable investment opportunities have been exhausted.

According to the free cash flow hypothesis, once the firm has terminated all the profitable investment opportunities available, agency conflicts between shareholders and managers could arise because the two parties might have different interests on the use and allocation of the residual cash flows.

On the one hand, shareholders demand direct payout of the firm's asset, either in the form of cash dividend payouts or share repurchases (Easterbrook, 1984; Jensen, 1988). On the other, managers are interested in keeping resources inside the firm under their direct control (Jensen, 1986, p. 323). Given that conflict, managers may have incentive to use any residual cash flow to finance negative net present value projects with low benefit for the shareholders (Jensen, 1986).

According to the Jensen's hypothesis, conflicts between shareholders and managers are stronger in firms with a combination of both high free cash flow and low growth prospects, while they are lower in firms with limited free cash flow and high growth prospects. However, agency conflicts between the managers and share-holders exist as long as the firm does not undertake specific remedies.

In this respect, Jensen (1986) argues that agency conflicts between shareholders and managers on the use of free cash flow can be mitigated by the firm through the issue of debt.

This hypothesis, called by Jensen as *"control hypothesis"* states that debt creation, without retention of the proceeds of the issue, enables managers effectively to bond their promise to pay out future cash flow (Jensen, 1986, p. 324). That is, by issuing debt, "managers give to shareholder-recipients of the debt the right to take the firm into bankruptcy court if they do not keep their promise to make the interest and principal payments" (Jensen, 1986, p. 324). In a context where the claim of the bondholders on free cash flow is stronger, the portion of free cash flow that is subject to managers' spending discretion is lower. Thus, Jensen concludes, *"these control effects of debt are a potential determinant of the capital structure"*.

Previous finance theory suggests that debt, despite providing tax advantages, can have noxious consequences for a firm, as it increases the risk of financial distress and the related expected bankruptcy costs (i.e., agency costs of debt). While acknowl-edging that debt financing is not without cost,[2] Jensen (1986) adds to this literature

---

[2] Jensen (1988, p. 30) clarifies this point: *"Increased leverage has costs. As leverage increases, the usual agency costs of debt, including bankruptcy costs, rise. The incentives to take on projects that reduce total firm value but benefit shareholders through a transfer of wealth from bondholders is*

arguing that, besides providing fiscal advantages, debt financing can also have a positive effect in mitigating agency conflicts between shareholders and managers. Specifically, the larger is the portion of free cash flow bounded for debt servicing purpose, the lower the portion of free cash flow available to the managers for lavish expenditures is. In such context, under the threat of failing debt repayments, managers are motivated to act efficiently in the interest of the shareholders. This effect is referred by Jensen under the name of *"agency benefits of debt"* or "(debt) *control hypothesis"* (a.k.a. *"debt monitoring hypothesis"*) (Jensen, 1986). Later empirical research has provided evidence confirming the role of debt as a moderator of agency conflicts (e.g., Harris & Raviv, 1988, 1991; Stulz, 1988; Rajan & Winton, 1995).

3.1.3 Agency Conflicts and Capital Structure

As previously discussed, the Agency Theory acknowledges the existence of two main sources of agency conflicts in a firm. A first source is represented by the conflict between managers (i.e., agents) and shareholders (i.e., principals). This form of agency conflicts is known as *Type I agency conflicts*. Type I agency conflicts arise because the separation of ownership and control could create information asymmetries between managers and shareholders (Bearle & Means, 1932; Jensen & Meckling, 1976). As a result, moral hazardous managers could engage in self-servicing activities (e.g., consumption of perquisites, overcompensation, and empire building) exclusively aimed at maximizing their personal wealth at the expenses of the shareholders. These activities may decrease the level of cash flow that is expected by the shareholders and, in turn, exacerbate the agency conflicts between managers and shareholders, increasing a firm's cost of capital and the associated financial risks (e.g., bond default and bankruptcy risk) (Ashbaugh-Skaife et al., 2006).

A second type of agency conflicts is the conflict that arises between shareholders (and managers) and bondholders. This form of agency conflict is also known as *Type II agency conflicts*. Type II agency conflicts can occur because, in high levered firms, shareholders might have incentive to take actions aimed at diverting bondholders' wealth (Galai & Masulis, 1976; Jensen & Meckling, 1976). These actions are made possible because the borrowers' behavior is partially unknown to the lender (Demerjian & Owens, 2016). As a result, borrowers (shareholders and managers) can take advantage from this situation at the bondholders' expenses. Creditors may partially anticipate the managers' moral hazard and attempting to alleviate it by requiring, ex-ante, specific debt contract contingencies (Platikanova, 2017). Debt covenants are one of the most common contract devices used to alleviate Type II

---

one source of these costs. These costs put a limit on the desirable level of debt. The optimal debt/ equity ratio is the point at which firm value is maximized, the point where marginal costs of debt just offset the marginal benefits [of debt]".

agency conflicts (Chava & Roberts, 2008; Demiroglu & James, 2010). By appointing debt covenants into debt contracts, the managers implicitly make the promise to avoid engaging in highly discretionary activities that are of little or no benefits for the bondholders (e.g., Nini et al., 2012; Ozelge & Saunders, 2012). Hence, the violation of debt covenants can be a significantly costly event for the firm and a source of personal costs for its managers (Dyreng et al., 2022).[3]

As for the agency conflict between shareholders and managers, even the conflict between shareholders (and managers) and bondholders can also have an important implication for a firm's corporate capital structure. In fact, if the shareholders achieve the managers' *placet* to invest in high-risk projects that increase the mean and variance of future cash flow (i.e., *asset substitution*),[4] the bondholders (i.e., fixed-claimants) will face a higher risk of default and will demand a higher cost of debt capital and/or stricter contract requirements such as stringent covenants and collaterals (Ashbaugh-Skaife et al., 2006, p. 6; Hasan et al., 2014). As a result, severe Type II agency conflicts are also likely to affect the corporate capital structure by increasing its cost, making the firm exposed to tighter debt covenants and, overall, increasing its default likelihood (Ashbaugh-Skaife et al., 2006).

In the Jensen's Agency framework (Jensen, 1986), however, the relations between managers and shareholders and that one between the shareholders and bondholders are not to be interpreted as isolated compartments. Yet, the relation between the shareholders and bondholders can influence that one between shareholders and managers. In this way, issuing more debt does not always coincide with an increase of Type II agency conflicts. Rather, as suggested by the Jensen's free cash flow hypothesis, as long as the agency costs of debt are not so high to offset its benefits, debt can have important moderating effect and being useful to stimulate managerial efficiency (Jensen, 1986). Therefore, the tighter is the bondholder's control on the firm's free cash flow, the lower the agency conflicts between the shareholders and managers (i.e., Type I agency conflict) will be. Implicitly, according to Jensen, there is an optimal leverage ratio which maximizes the control benefits of debt (and its related tax advantages) and minimizes the related agency costs (i.e., Type II Agency conflicts). This optimal debt-equity ratio, in the author's own words, is *"the point where the marginal costs of debt just offset the marginal benefits"* (Jensen, 1986, p. 324).

---

[3]Consistently, prior accounting and finance literature shows that the proximity of to the covenant violation can be a trigger for managers' discretion, which can take the form of several "window dressing" activities likely to be detrimental for the quality of a firm's financial reports (Kothari et al., 2005; Roychowdhury, 2006; Alissa et al., 2013; Dyreng et al., 2022).

[4]Asset substitution refers to risk-shifting activities resulting in expropriation of wealth by shareholders (and managers) at debtholders' expenses (Galai & Masulis, 1976; Jensen & Meckling, 1976; Eisdorfer, 2008). Asset substitution can create agency costs that influence the cost and structure of capital and the associated level of financial distress. Consistently, several studies found that agency costs related to asset substitution can result in a reduction of the debt maturity and an increase of loan spreads (Smith & Watts, 1992; Leland, 1998; Rajan & Zingales, 1995; Morellec, 2004).

Drawing on the Agency Theory, Vos and Forlong (1996) suggest that the expected tax advantage and agency cost (and advantage) from debt is likely to be different across the life cycle stage of a firm. Each stage of a firm life cycle is associated with different level of interests' alignment between the managers and the shareholders and to different business fundamentals which may interact with the expected benefits and costs from debt. Therefore, the expected tax and non-tax advantage (cost) of debt is also likely to vary across each different stage. In the early stages of the corporate life cycle, the expected benefit from debt is likely to be limited and usually outweighed by the related costs (i.e., financial distress costs). Start-up firms are usually featured by a limited degree of separation between ownership and control and by negative taxable income. Debt is unlikely to provide significant monitoring advantage in this phase. Conversely, when the firm reach maturity, the advantages related to debt financing are likely to outweigh the related cost. With limited risk of bankruptcy in this stage, higher separation between ownership and control, and positive taxable income, mature firms are more likely to exploit both the agency and tax benefits of debt financing. On the one hand, debt can help reducing agency conflicts between the shareholders and managers, especially in firms with a limited quality of their corporate governance structures. On the other the firm can benefit from passive interests from debt financing to reduce its tax burden and enhance profitability.

3.2   The Agency Theory of Tax Avoidance

The theory of corporate tax avoidance in an Agency setting grounds its roots in the theoretical economics of tax evasion (e.g., Allingham & Sandmo, 1972) and on coeval contributions in the field of Economics of criminal activities (Becker, 1968; Tulkens & Jacquemin, 1971), and Economics of uncertainty (Mossin, 1968; Arrow, 1971).

Allingham and Sandmo (1972) were the first to provide a comprehensive analytical framework to explain personal tax evasion. According to their framework, the individual engagement in tax evasion can be explained as the result of four major drivers, namely: (1) the tax rates; (2) the probability of detention and punishment; (3) penalties; (4) the level of risk-aversion.[5]

Although the Allingham-Sandmo's framework is meant to describe the personal tax avoidance (and compliance) behavior, scholars suggest that similar factors can also be useful to explain the corporate tax avoidance behavior (Hanlon & Heitzman, 2010). Notwithstanding, other relevant factors need to be acknowledged when examining tax evasion or tax avoidance at a corporate level.

---

[5] See, also, Hanlon and Heitzman (2010) on this point. A potential additional motivation can be the taxpayer's intrinsic motivation, such as, for example, civic duty considerations (Hanlon & Heitzman, 2010).

In "*The Economics of Corporate Tax Selfishness*", Slemrod (2004) indicates that any theoretical framework aiming to describe tax avoidance in a corporate setting should take in consideration the impact of agency conflicts stemming from the separation between ownership and control. Starting from Slemrod (2004), the Agency Theory has received a central position in the corporate tax avoidance research. Later publications furtherly contributed to develop the Agency framework in a tax setting (e.g., Chen & Chu, 2005; Crocker & Slemrod, 2005; Desai et al., 2007; Desai & Dharmapala, 2009).

Chen and Chu (2005) were the first to examine managers' compensation in presence of owners-led corporate income tax evasion. Basing on the analytical framework developed, the Authors suggest that, although corporate income tax evasion might increase the firm's level of after-tax profit, such beneficial effect could be offset by a loss of internal control efficiency.[6] Crocker and Slemrod (2005) furtherly delve in deep the agency framework elaborated by Chen and Chu, by focusing, in this case, on the peculiar role played by tax managers. According to the authors, tax managers deserve a special attention when examining corporate tax avoidance. Indeed, among the firms' managers, tax managers are the only one to be endowed with private information on the legal and illegal tax shelters. Moreover, differently to the other corporate executives, tax managers are typically tied to the firms through contracts that reward their success in minimizing tax expenditures. Thus, most of the firm's tax avoidance conduct can be better interpreted by considering the functions and contractual incentives set by the shareholders to the tax managers. Basing on these considerations, Crocker and Slemrod (2005) suggest that tax minimization incentives to the tax managers set by the shareholders can lose their power if the tax manager is subject to penalties in the case of tax allegation. In line with this finding, the authors conclude that agency-based penalties assessed on the tax managers, rather than on the corporation, are the most effective mean to mitigate corporate tax evasion (tax avoidance). This result can have important policy consequences and can suggest why a *sic et simpliciter* stricter tax enforcement could not always lead to the expected results.[7]

Desai and Dharmapala (2006) provide additional investigation on the link between corporate tax avoidance and executives' incentives. The Authors find that incentive compensations are negatively associated with the level of tax avoidance. The negative relation between incentive compensation and tax avoidance is consistent with the idea of a complementarity between tax sheltering and rent diversion.

---

[6]In their own words, the authors stated: "*Our model implies that although a risk-neutral individual will evade taxes if and only if expected profit from evasion is greater than that from reporting honestly, a risk-neutral owner of firm will evade tax only when the expected profit from evasion is greater than that from reporting honestly by a substantial margin. Even if the expected tax savings from evasion is positive and the principal is risk neutral, she will not necessarily choose to evade taxes, i.e., the condition for profitable tax evasion is more stringent for firms than for individuals, because efficiency loss may outweigh the expected gain*" (Chen & Chu, 2005, p. 152).

[7]A compelling discussion on the relation between tax enforcement and tax avoidance can be found in Hoopes et al. (2012).

Therefore, according to the Authors' argument, in companies where there are strong incentive compensation schemes for the tax managers, a lower level of corporate tax avoidance can be expected. Findings of Desai and Dharmapala (2006) suggest the existence of an interplay between corporate tax avoidance and corporate governance structures. In a later study, Desai et al. (2007) provide in-depth examination of such connection.

The paper of Desai et al. (2007), entitled *"Theft and Taxes"*, is regarded by tax scholars as a milestone in the context of the agency theoretical corporate tax avoidance literature (see Hanlon & Heitzman, 2010). While this study is not without limitations (see e.g., Armstrong et al., 2015; Blaylock, 2016 for a critique of the complementarity between tax avoidance and rent extraction), it offers some important insights on the complementarity between tax avoidance and governance structures. According to the authors, a main reason why corporate tax avoidance and corporate governance are so intimately connected is that most of the transactions aimed at diverting corporate value also reduce corporate tax liabilities. At the same time, most of procedures aiming at enforcing a corporate tax liability could make difficult the diversion of corporate value (Desai et al., 2007, p. 592).

Another relevant novelty of the analysis provided by Desai et al. (2007) is that of integrating the role of the State (i.e., tax authority) in the examination of the link between corporate tax avoidance and corporate governance. Specifically, the authors conjectured that *"the state, thanks to its claim on cash flow, is* de facto, *the largest minority shareholders in almost all corporations"*. Therefore, the analysis of the corporate tax avoidance behavior in an agency-setting should consider the role played by the state in the vest of tax authority. A major consequence of this assumption is that of interpreting the level of rent diversion and the amount of taxes paid as the result of a game involving three different parties, namely: the state in the guise of tax authority, the insider, and outside shareholders (Desai et al., 2007). Hence—the authors suggest—any bilateral interaction among each of these parties can have important spillover effects on the third party.

For example, the state's level of tax enforcement and the design of the fiscal system can have spillover effects on the relationship between insider and outside shareholders. Namely, the higher (lower) is the tax rate, the more (less) is the level of rent extracted by the firm's insiders. In turn, this condition could worsen (improve) the relation between insiders and outside shareholders and, thus, being detrimental (positive) for the quality of corporate governance. Conversely, a tax enforcement crackdown could increase the outside shareholders' wealth, and, together with it, the company's market value.

Finally, another interesting aspect of the model developed by Desai et al. (2007) is that of allowing for a specular interpretation. Specifically, since the external macroeconomic inputs (i.e., the tax rate and the design of the fiscal system) can influence the internal firms' corporate governance mechanism, at the same time, the internal firms' corporate governance characteristics are also likely to influence the external macroeconomic outcome (i.e., the amount of taxes paid by the companies). Namely, in presence of strong corporate governance mechanisms (i.e., when diverting income is not easy), an increase in the tax rate can increase tax revenues. On the contrary, in presence of weak corporate governance mechanisms (i.e., when diverting income is easier), an increase in the tax rate can reduces tax revenues (Desai et al., 2007, p. 592).

Overall, a major notion that emerges from Desai et al. (2007) and later from Desai and Dharmapala (2009) is that, in a context where shareholders and managers interests are aligned, managers will be likely to behave like "residual claimants" and, thus, engaging in tax avoidance to improve shareholders' wealth. According to this view, tax avoidance aimed at increasing firm's value arises in business context where the interests of shareholders and those of managers are aligned. However, since the interests of managers are often not perfectly aligned with the interests of shareholders, managers could still engage in tax avoidance strategies to pursue self-servicing activities and/or being reluctant to pursue value-increasing tax minimization strategies. Desai and Dharmapala (2009) describe the activity of obfuscation necessary to shield income from the tax authority and those related to rent extraction as complementary diversion technologies (Desai & Dharmapala, 2009).

3.3 Tax Avoidance and Capital Structure in a Principal-Agent Perspective

Despite the theoretical advancements in the field of corporate tax avoidance, as Hanlon and Heitzman (2010) noted, "(. . .) *the theory of corporate tax avoidance in an agency framework is relatively young and is not well developed or sufficiently incorporated in the empirical literature at this time*". Therefore, different competing predictions on the association between tax avoidance and corporate capital structure can be drawn basing on the Agency Theory. Lee et al. (2022) argue that tax avoidance, given its effect on the expected cash flow, affects all the other financial choices since it alters the relative cost of debt and equity. However, given its effect on the firm's cash flow, as previously discussed, tax avoidance can also impact on the level of present and future agency conflicts (Jensen, 1986; Ashbaugh-Skaife et al., 2006). Therefore, the impact of tax avoidance on the cost and on the composition of the capital structure cannot be longer explained in light of a purely mechanical association of tax avoidance with the other sources of capital.[8] So far, the literature on the relationship between tax avoidance and capital structure in the presence of owners-managers agency conflicts has provided two competing views.

---

[8]In Chap. 2, I have explained the potential implications of tax avoidance on the cost of capital in a context in which agency conflicts are not considered. In such context, the effect of tax avoidance on the cost of capital and the related financial default risk can be explained as the result of a mechanical effect of tax avoidance on the other sources of financing. Here, I provide a theoretical explanation of the effect of tax avoidance on the cost of capital and financial default risk in a context where Type I agency conflicts (i.e., agency conflicts between shareholders and managers) are duly taken in account.

According to a first set of studies, the separation between corporate shareholders (i.e., principal) and managers (i.e., agents) can prompt managers to use tax avoidance as a vehicle through which maximizing their personal utility at the expenses of shareholders (i.e., the *"tunneling"* view) (e.g., Dhaliwal et al., 2011; Atwood & Lewellen, 2019). Although tax avoidance consists in a hijack of resources from the government to the shareholders, these studies suggest that, in context of high Type I agency conflicts, tax avoidance can create an opaque business environment that facilitates managerial opportunistic behavior, rent extraction, and rent diversion (e.g., Desai & Dharmapala, 2006, 2009; Desai et al., 2007; Wilson, 2009). Therefore, both the government and shareholders' interests could result penalized by tax avoidance activities. In line with this view, prior studies show that a higher level of tax avoidance increases the firm's cost of capital and its related bankruptcy risk owing to rent diversion, opaque financial reporting, and sub-optimal allocation of cash resources (Desai & Dharmapala, 2006; Green & Kerr, 2022; Dhaliwal et al., 2011; Noga & Schnader, 2013; Dhawan et al., 2020). Moreover, since rent diversion related to tax avoidance can also result in higher information asymmetries and moral hazard (Lim, 2011b), capital market participants can negatively react to firms' tax avoidance. For example, bondholders (i.e., *fixed claimants*) may not expect to benefit from tax avoidance and can perceive these activities as a risky (Hasan et al., 2014; Platikanova, 2017; Shevlin et al., 2020). As a result, bondholders could react to corporate tax avoidance by increasing loan spreads and asking tax avoider firms for more frequent renegotiation of their debt positions (Hasan et al., 2014; Platikanova, 2017). Equity-holders (i.e., *residual claimants*), at the same time, although potentially beneficiaries of tax avoidance activities (Goh et al., 2016), could perceive tax avoidance as a signal of managerial rent extraction and bad news hoarding by managers (Kim et al., 2011).

On the other hand, a second stream of the literature indicates that tax avoidance is a value-increasing activity and that could lead to a lower cost of capital, a lower debt covenant violation likelihood, and to a lower risk of default (Desai & Dharmapala, 2009; Kim et al., 2010; Goh et al., 2016; Bayar et al., 2018; Hasan et al., 2021). Consistent with this view (i.e., the *"value-enhancing"* view), this second stream of literature suggests that, in context with low Type I agency conflicts, shareholders may deliberately incentivize managers to pursue efficient tax minimization strategies (Phillips, 2003). Additional cash flow from tax avoidance could be directed to the repayment of firms' debt positions, to reward firms' shareholders in the form of cash dividend payouts or to be retained in the firm in the form of precautionary cash holdings. Guenther et al. (2020) and Heitzman and Lester (2021) show that firms typically employ cash savings from tax avoidance to create cash cushions useful to minimize the risk of future events. In a similar way, Richardson et al. (2015) show that Australian public firms used tax avoidance as an additional source of funds during the global financial crisis. Basing on Lambert et al. (2007), Goh et al. (2016) also suggest that, given the positive effect of tax avoidance on the expected cash flow, the cost of equity capital of the firms engaging in tax avoidance is lower than those more tax compliant. Overall, this literature indicates that precautionary and value-increasing motives are a relevant reason for using tax avoidance. Cash savings from tax avoidance could be used to crowd-out other costlier source of funds (i.e., financial debt) (Graham & Tucker, 2006; Law & Mills, 2015; Edwards et al., 2016). Therefore, a higher level of tax avoidance is likely to be associated with a lower cost of capital, a lower debt covenant violation risk, and to a lower risk of default (Graham & Tucker, 2006; Kim et al., 2010; Bayar et al., 2018).

In the following paragraphs, under the guidance of the Jensen's free cash flow hypothesis (Jensen, 1986), the relationship between tax avoidance and capital structuring is disentangled in its main drivers (see Sect. 3.4). The Chapter, then, concludes with a special focus on debt covenants, as they represent a critical feature of the firms' agency-driven debt contracting and core aspect of the capital structure management of many firms (see Sect. 3.5).

3.4 Tax Avoidance and Capital Structure: Free Cash Flow vs. Agency Benefits of Debt

Drawing on the Jensen's free cash flow hypothesis (Jensen, 1986), and considering the relationship of tax avoidance with the other capital structure decisions (DeAngelo & Masulis, 1980), this paragraph provides a conceptual framework developed which can help explaining the relation between tax avoidance and the capital structure. Specifically, it is argued that the implications of tax avoidance activities for a firm's capital structure can be interpreted as the endogenous result of three distinct mechanisms, namely: (a) a *"free cash flow effect"*; (b) a *"debt substitution effect"*; (c) a *"debt monitoring effect"*.

3.4.1 The Free Cash Flow Effect

Jensen's free cash flows hypothesis (Jensen, 1986) suggests that firms with higher agency conflicts between managers and shareholders are those having, on average, more pronounced free cash flow, lower growth prospects, and limited portions of free cash flow subject to the bondholders' claims (Jensen, 1986). In such a context, managers are likely to undertake non-value maximizing activities and to invest in negative present value projects (i.e., *over-investment*),[9] instead of disgorging cash towards shareholders in the form of cash dividend payouts (Jensen, 1986, 1988, 1989; Jaggi & Gul, 1999).

---

[9]Overinvestment can be defined as "investment expenditure beyond that required to maintain the assets in place or to finance expected new investments in positive net present value projects" (Richardson, 2006). In this respect, Khurana et al. (2018) find that tax avoidance is positively associated with overinvestment, consistently with a tax avoidance incremental effect on the agency conflicts on free cash flow.

Jensen defines the free cash flow as "the cash flow in excess of that required to fund all projects that have positive net present values when discounted at the relevant cost of capital (Jensen, 1986, p. 323)". As such, the firm's free cash flow is the "cash flow beyond what is necessary to maintain assets in place and to finance expected new investments" (Richardson, 2006, p. 160). Basing on the Jensen's free cash flow hypothesis, Richardson (2006) suggests that potential squander of free cash flow is possible only in firms with a positive free cash flow. In a world without market frictions, firms could satisfy their need for additional cash resources through external capital markets. In such a world, any excess of cash beyond the amount needed to finance all profitable investment projects, would be distributed externally in the form of dividend payouts. However, since firms operate in a world with market frictions, firms are incentivized to satisfy their need for additional cash resources by using internally generated cash resources (e.g., cash tax savings from tax avoidance). As a result, any excess of cash beyond the amount needed to finance all profitable investment projects would be used to finance management self-servicing projects instead of being used to increase the shareholders' value (Richardson, 2006).

Tax avoidance can have a substantial appositive effect on the firm's free cash flow, since it increases the firm's level of operating (after-tax) cash flow (Penman & Penman, 2010; Ayers et al., 2018; Guenther et al., 2020; Asiri et al., 2020). There is broad empirical support for such an effect in the literature. For example, findings from Ayers et al. (2018) suggest that tax avoidance can be a significant operating cash flow-enhancing activity. By examining the effect of the analysts' use of cash flow forecasts on the firm's improvement of its cash flow through tax avoidance, the authors find that cash savings from tax avoidance are responsible for approximately 56% of the increased firm's reported operating cash flow of profitable firms. Guenther et al. (2020) move this literature front on, by exploring how the internal cash flow of firms that pay less taxes are allocated. The Authors find that tax avoidance increases the balance of operating cash flow. Moreover, by using a flow-of-funds model derived from Finance studies (i.e., Chang et al., 2014), they also find that tax-related operating cash flows are allocated on different bases than other non-tax related operating cash flow. This result is consistent with the unique risk affecting tax-related cash flow, including, for example, the threat of future penalties. Despite such risk, however, findings from Huang et al. (2016) suggest that generation of internal source of funds through tax avoidance is relatively cheap, especially in firms having a high concentrated costumers' structure. The relatively cheapness may justify why firms rely on tax avoidance as an additional source of financing when severely distressed or in period of economic crisis (Brondolo, 2009). Consistently, a plethora of studies provide evidence that tax avoidance activities can represent an effective source of funds for firms facing internal financial constraints and/or the negative consequences of adverse macroeconomic conditions, thus suggesting a certain economic convenience for firms to use tax avoidance (Mills & Newberry, 2001; Noga & Schnader, 2013; Richardson et al., 2015; Law & Mills, 2015; Edwards et al., 2016; Bayar et al., 2018; Akamah et al., 2021).

3.4.2   The Debt Substitution Effect

As already discussed at Chap. 2, the DeAngelo and Masulis (1980) hypothesis suggests that firms use non-debt tax shields (e.g., tax avoidance/tax sheltering) as a substitute for debt tax shields. Later empirical evidence suggests that, consistently with the DeAngelo and Masulis's prediction, changes in the level of non-debt tax shields can explain the cross-sectional variation of corporate debt policies (e.g., MacKie-Mason, 1990; Graham et al., 2004; Graham & Tucker, 2006; Wilson, 2009; Lim, 2011a, 2011b; Lin et al., 2014; Goh et al., 2016; De Vito & Jacob, 2021; Lee et al., 2022). Clearly, both debt and non-debt tax shields can produce tax advantages. However, the tax advantage of any type of tax shields is realized only when the firm has a positive taxable income. Both the classes of tax shields compete for being deducted against the firm's taxable income. Therefore, set equal the level of tax benefit achievable from such deduction, the firm will prefer the tax shields that minimize the cost for its realization.

Besides the potential tax advantage related to the interest deductions, debt can also bound the firm to future fixed payments to the borrowers, in addition to increase its likelihood of financial distress (Graham, 2000, 2003). Hence, in presence of non-debt tax shields, firms may be willing to marginally reduce their debt positions to take fiscal advantage of any additional non-debt tax shields outstanding the level of debt tax shields (MacKie-Mason, 1990; Trezevant, 1992; Graham, 1996; Graham & Tucker, 2006).

Trezevant (1992) shows that the firm's increased probability of losing the opportunity to use debt tax shields triggers the decision to reduce the level of debt, consistent with a tax exhaustion hypothesis. Similarly, Graham and Tucker (2006) suggest that when the firm has so many non-debt tax shields that completely offset the taxable income, the firm will be unable to use all its interest tax deduction. As a result, the more a firm is close to exhaust the base of taxable income deductibility, the higher the likelihood that the firm will prefer non-debt tax shields over additional debt tax shields is.

In such a case, the benefit arising from reducing the debt (e.g., reduction of expected bankruptcy costs) is higher than the potential tax advantage related to the interest deduction, which can now be achieved using non-debt tax shields. Consistently with this reasoning, Graham (1996) suggests that the crowding-out effect between the two classes of tax shields is particularly evident in financially distressed firms, where the advantage of reducing debt is considerable, and the portion of taxable income deductible generally limited (Graham, 1996).

3.4.3   The Debt Monitoring Effect

The Jensen's free cash flow hypothesis suggests that debt may be used by firms to reduce the agency conflicts between shareholders and managers. Jensen refers to this effect as "control hypothesis for debt creation" (Jensen, 1986, p. 324). The "control hypothesis for debt creation" or "debt-monitoring hypothesis" (a.k.a., "agency benefits of debt") states that debt creation (without the retention of the proceeds of the issue) "enables managers to effectively bond their promise to pay out cash. Thus, debt can be an effective substitute for dividends (...). By issuing debt in exchange for stock, managers are bonding their promise to pay out future cash flows in a way that cannot be accomplished by simple dividend increases". Therefore, according to Jensen, "debt reduces the agency costs of free cash flow by reducing the cash flow available at the discretion of managers" (Jensen, 1986, p. 324). According to corporate finance literature, the debt-monitoring effect is determined not only because debt can signal shareholders of a firm's willingness to pay out cash flows, but also because debt can implicitly express the firm's *placet* to be monitored by its lenders/bondholders, even without the intervention of the capital market (Leland & Pyle, 1977; Ross, 1977; Flannery, 1986; Diamond, 1991; see: Harvey et al., 2004, p. 5).

Focusing on firms with extreme agency conflicts (i.e., emerging market firms with pyramid ownership structures), Harvey et al. (2004) test whether debt could mitigate agency conflicts. The authors find that debt increases are positively associated with the shareholders' value, consistent with debt acting in a similar way to corporate governance mechanisms even in most refractory business environment.

If a higher level of debt mitigates the agency conflict between shareholders and managers on the free cash flow, then a higher level of tax avoidance is likely to increase the agency conflicts between shareholders and managers not only because it mechanically increases the portion of free cash flow available to managers (i.e., the "free cash flow effect"), but also because it could implicitly waive the firm from the control of its bondholders due to the substitution effect. This, at least partially, could explain why tax avoidance firms face on average higher financing costs, more frequent debt renegotiation, and is subject, on average, to more stringent collateral and debt covenants than other tax compliant firms (Hasan et al., 2014; Platikanova, 2017). In this sense, it is thus reasonable to expect, that as long as the agency benefits associated with the debt outweigh the related agency costs, a higher level of tax avoidance can exacerbate the agency conflicts on the free cash flow for reason that are beyond the free cash flow effect. Hence, all else being equal, a negative association between tax avoidance and the bondholders' monitoring power could be expected.

3.5   Tax Avoidance and Capital Structure: A Focus on Debt Covenants

3.5.1   The Role of Debt Covenants in the Capital Structure and the Risks of Their Violation

Debt covenants are a crucial aspect of the capital management of many firms and play a key rule within the managerial capital structure decision-making (Dichev & Skinner, 2002). Prior literature defines debt covenants as binding clauses demanding the debtor to satisfy specific accounting-based requirements (e.g., a minimum level of interest coverage or a maximum Debt-to-EBITDA).[10] The Agency Theory provides the theoretical framework through which explaining the existence of debt covenants in debt agreements. According to the Agency Theory of Covenants (also referred to as "ACT" or "Debt Covenant Hypothesis"), in a bank loan contract, debt covenants serve at mitigating the agency costs borne by the lender, protecting them from potential managerial discretion and information asymmetries (Roberts & Sufi, 2009; Franz et al., 2014). The ACT directly stems from the seminal contribution of Jensen and Meckling (1976) and have received important extension in later works by Myers (1977) and Smith Jr and Warner (1979).

The core "building concept" of the ACT is the assumption that the relationship between the managers (and their shareholders) and the corporate creditors is afflicted by information asymmetries, opportunistic behaviors, and potentially harmful discretion. Prior finance literature indicates at least two main issues associated in the relationship between the borrower and the lender when debt contracting, namely: (1) asset substitution, and (2) underinvestment Jensen & Meckling, 1976; Myers, 1977). The first refers to the incentive by the shareholders, through their influence over the management, to invest in riskier projects that can be harmful for fixed-claimant bondholders. The latter, also referred to as "debt overhang problem", consists in the possibility that the firm may forego potential investment opportunities with an expected net benefit for the bondholders (Platikanova, 2017). Although the bondholders may likely anticipate managers' risk-shifting activities, substantial information asymmetries and/or particularly high monitoring costs may prompt them to rely on ex-ante contracting devices aimed at addressing managerial discretion. Such devises may be distinguished between priced devices (i.e., the request of higher loan spreads) and non-priced devices (i.e., establishment of ex-ante contract contingencies). Among the most common contract contingencies, we can mention: (1) seniority status of cash flow claims; (2) debt covenants; (3) collaterals; and the (4) debt maturity choice (see: Platikanova, 2017). Debt covenants have an especially well-established application in debt contracting of public firms and are considered among the most used contracting device (Chava & Roberts, 2008; Billett et al., 2007;

---

[10] See Demerjian and Owens (2016) for a detailed list of the mostly used debt covenant, their definitions and their frequency in debt contracting.

Table 3.1 Covenant standard definitions and frequencies based on Demerjian and Owens (2016)

Financial covenant	Standard definition	Frequency (%)
Min. interest coverage	EBITDA/interest expense	76.3
Min. cash interest coverage	EBITDA/interest paid	76.8
Min. fixed charge coverage	EBITDA/(interest expense + principal + rent expense)	2.7
Min. debt service coverage	EBITDA/(Interest expense + principal)	37.9
Max debt-to-EBITDA	Debt/EBITDA	91.0
Max. senior debt-to-EBITDA	Senior debt/EBITDA	89.4
Max. leverage	Debt/assets	84.5
Max. senior leverage	Senior debt/assets	86.8
Max. debt-to-tangible net worth	Debt/TNW	52.9
Max. debt-to-equity	Debt/NW	47.6
Min. current ratio	Current assets/current liabilities	95.4
Min. quick ratio	Account receivable + cash and equivalents/current liabilities	66.7
Min. EBITDA	EBITDA	97.4
Min net worth	NW	33.7[a]/96.9[b]
Min. tangible net worth	TNW	32.5[a]/99.5[b]

Notes: [a], [b]Considering (excluding) the effect of escalators. The frequency is commeasured basing on the sample of firms examined in Demerjian and Owens (2016)
Source: Author's adaptation from Demerjian and Owens (2016)

Demiroglu & James, 2010). Table 3.1 reports a synthetic list of common financial covenants definition used in debt contracting practices and their frequencies within debt agreements.

By writing debt covenants, as those listed before, the managers, thus, implicitly make the promise to avoid engaging high risk activities that can be detrimental for the lenders' interests (Malitz, 1986; Begley & Feltham, 1999; Bradley & Roberts, 2015). Scholars find that firms making extensive use of debt covenants increase their access to debt financing with lower financing costs (Reisel, 2014). Hence, the violation of a debt covenant (a.k.a "technical default") is likely to be costly event for the firm (i.e., borrower) and its managers, as it allows the lenders to exercise their contractual rights (Dyreng et al., 2022).

Prior debt covenant literature show that there exists a robust and positive relationship between the violation of a debt covenant and the firm's cost-of-capital (Gao et al., 2017; Butt, 2019). This literature indicates that debt covenant violation may affect the corporate capital structure in at least two important ways. On the one hand, the violation of a debt covenant triggers information asymmetries (i.e., agency conflicts) between the managers and the lenders, nullifying the promise made by the managers to abstain from engaging potentially harmful risky activities. On the other, violating debt covenants may also increase the volatility of firm's expected returns, increasing the shareholders uncertainty and, with it, the required cost of capital (Gao et al., 2017; Roberts & Sufi, 2009). Nini et al. (2012) finds that after covenants violation the loans exhibit higher spreads and shorter maturity. Freudenberg et al. (2017) also show stricter loan contract terms for violator companies, consistent with borrowers bearing a stigma for the violation. Butt (2019) confirms the positive relationship between debt covenant violation and the cost-of-capital, showing that violators are typically burdened by higher costs when raising new debt from the market. Several anecdotal evidence also show that violation of debt covenants may raise a "red flag" for rating agencies, triggering credit rating downgrades which increase the firm's risk of default. Since capital market participants usually react to debt covenant violation by timely modifying their risk-adjusted expected cash flow, such events are likely to promptly affect the firm's cost of capital and to be hardly reversible in the short-term. Freudenberg et al. (2017) show that the probability of default for an average covenant violator firm is expected to increase of more than 6% in the first 10 days after the violation and to slowly reverse to a pre-violation level in more than 80 days. Within the corporate capital structure management, then, real events like debt covenant violation can, thus, provide a unique setting in which the corporate capital structure of the firm (and its related cost) is directly affected by the agency conflicts (Easley, & O'Hara, 2004; Tirole, 2006; Roberts & Sufi, 2009).[11]

3.5.2 *Accounting and Tax Discretion as Violation Preventing Tools*

Prior accounting and finance literature show that the violation of a debt covenant is a highly costly event for the firm and its managers. Costs of violating a debt covenant are either direct or indirect and can take the form of refinancing costs (i.e., higher interest expenses), renegotiation and restructuring costs, and personal costs for the executives (Beneish & Press, 1993, 1995). Aiming at avoiding such costs and to satisfy lenders' requirements, managers may be willing to use accounting discretion and to engage in several "window dressing" activities (e.g., DeFond & Jiambalvo, 1994; Dichev & Skinner, 2002; Franz et al., 2014). Extant research primarily focused on earnings management, providing evidence of income manipulation around debt covenant violation (DeAngelo et al., 1994; Rosner, 2003; Charitou et al., 2007). However, this literature has provided conflicting evidence, so far. On the one hand, some studies found that firms are likely to engage in upward income

---

[11] These events are expected to affect the overall cost-of-capital both by the channel of the cost of debt and from that on related to the cost of equity capital. On the one hand, higher information asymmetries between the debtor and the lenders and lower credit ratings can make refinancing and renegotiation costs higher, thus increasing the firm's cost of debt. On the other, corporate shareholders will require a higher cost of equity capital, owning to the higher default risk.

manipulation activities as the proximity to the violation increases (e.g., Rosner, 2003). On the other hand, scholars provide evidence of downward earning management before violating a debt covenant (e.g., DeAngelo et al., 1994; Charitou et al., 2007). While not all the downward earnings management activities are motivated by tax purposes (i.e., tax-induced earnings management), tax avoidance could partially explain these mixed evidence (Badertscher et al., 2009). Hence, an investigation of the effect tax avoidance strategies on the likelihood of debt covenant violation is of utmost importance to extend this line of research.

Particularly, understanding whether tax avoidance increases or reduce the debt covenant violation likelihood, as conditioned by the life cycle stages of a firm, can be of interest for at least two main reasons. First, most of prior literature examining the consequences of tax avoidance for the corporate capital structure has primarily focused on the cost of debt capital and the cost of equity capital separately, overlooking investigation on real events affecting the capital structure of a firm, like debt covenant violation, potentially related with both of them. The debt covenant violation can provide a unique "channel" by which the entire corporate capital structure of the firm in directly affected by agency conflicts (Roberts & Sufi, 2009). Further, as a real event, compared to other capital structure contingencies, the identification of debt covenant violation is based on publicly and objectively identifiable information that are unlikely to be afflicted by measurement bias and/or ex-post blended approximation like traditional cost-of-capital proxies (i.e., the WACC) (Beaver et al., 2011).

Second, the (unpublished) research of Kim et al. (2010) that examined relationship between tax avoidance and debt covenant violation does not consider that different agency settings, as framed by the life cycle stages of a firms, may moderate such relationship. Kim et al. (2010) show that tax avoidance may act as a credit enhancing tool, avoiding the risk of covenant violation. However, recent tax research indicate that the motivation and aims of corporate tax avoidance activities may change across a firm's life cycle (Hasan et al., 2017). Prior studies investigating the implications of tax avoidance for a firm's cost-of-capital and the associated risk of default provided conflicting evidence so far (Graham & Tucker, 2006; Noga & Schnader, 2013; Shevlin et al., 2020; Dhawan et al., 2020). Hence, an investigation of the relationship between tax avoidance and the debt covenant violation likelihood across the firm's life cycle stages can be of interest for both theoretical and practical considerations. Theoretically, a specific focus on debt covenants can help to move the aforementioned literature front by focusing on a relatively overlooked aspect of the firm's capital structure management and providing, at least in part, a potential reconciliation of prior mixed evidence. Practically, a focus on the implications of tax avoidance for the debt covenant violation can also yield useful practical implications for the managers. Prior literature indicates that debt covenant violation can be an early warning signal of financial distress and of later increases of a firm's cost-of-capital (Habib et al., 2020). Therefore, a better understanding on whether tax avoidance practices are advantageous (or not) to avoid or delay such costly events can provide the managers with timely information on the benefits and risks of their tax strategies for the firm's financial health.

References

Akamah, H. T., Omer, T. C., & Shu, S. Q. (2021). Financial constraints and future tax outcome volatility. *Journal of Business Finance and Accounting, 48*(3–4), 637–665.

Alchian, A. A., & Demsetz, H. (1972). Production, information costs, and economic organization. *The American Economic Review, 62*(5), 777–795.

Alissa, W., Bonsall Iv, S. B., Koharki, K., & Penn, M. W., Jr. (2013). Firms' use of accounting discretion to influence their credit ratings. *Journal of Accounting and Economics, 55*(2–3), 129–147.

Allingham, M. G., & Sandmo, A. (1972). Income tax evasion: A theoretical analysis. *Taxation: Critical Perspectives on the World Economy, 3*, 323–338.

Armstrong, C. S., Blouin, J. L., Jagolinzer, A. D., & Larcker, D. F. (2015). Corporate governance, incentives, and tax avoidance. *Journal of Accounting and Economics, 60*(1), 1–17.

Arrow, K. J. (1971). *Insurance, risk and resource allocation.* University of Illinois at Urbana-Champaign's Academy for Entrepreneurial Leadership Historical Research Reference in Entrepreneurship.

Ashbaugh-Skaife, H., Collins, D. W., & LaFond, R. (2006). The effects of corporate governance on firms' credit ratings. *Journal of Accounting and Economics, 42*(1–2), 203–243.

Asiri, M., Al-Hadi, A., Taylor, G., & Duong, L. (2020). Is corporate tax avoidance associated with investment efficiency? *The North American Journal of Economics and Finance, 52*, 101143.

Atwood, T. J., & Lewellen, C. (2019). The complementarity between tax avoidance and manager diversion: Evidence from tax haven firms. *Contemporary Accounting Research, 36*(1), 259–294.

Ayers, B. C., Call, A. C., & Schwab, C. M. (2018). Do analysts' cash flow forecasts encourage managers to improve the firm's cash flows? Evidence from tax planning. *Contemporary Accounting Research, 35*(2), 767–793.

Badertscher, B. A., Phillips, J. D., Pincus, M., & Rego, S. O. (2009). Earnings management strategies and the trade-off between tax benefits and detection risk: To conform or not to conform? *The Accounting Review, 84*(1), 63–97.

Barnard, C. (1938). *The functions of the executive.* Harvard University Press.

Bayar, O., Huseynov, F., & Sardarli, S. (2018). Corporate governance, tax avoidance, and financial constraints. *Financial Management, 47*(3), 651–677.

Bearle, A., & Means, G. (1932). *The modern corporation and private property.* Macmillan.

Beaver, W. H., Correia, M., & McNichols, M. F. (2011). Financial statement analysis and the prediction of financial distress. *Foundations and Trends® in Accounting, 5*(2), 99–173.

Becker, G. S. (1968). Crime and punishment: An economic approach. In *The economic dimensions of crime* (pp. 13–68). Palgrave Macmillan.

Begley, J., & Feltham, G. A. (1999). An empirical examination of the relation between debt contracts and management incentives. *Journal of Accounting and Economics, 27*(2), 229–259.

Bendickson, J., Muldoon, J., Liguori, E. W., & Davis, P. E. (2016). Agency theory: The times, they are a changing. *Management Decision, 54*(1), 174–193.

Beneish, M. D., & Press, E. (1993). Costs of technical violation of accounting-based debt covenants. *The Accounting Review, 68*(2), 233–257.

Beneish, M. D., & Press, E. (1995). The resolution of technical default. *The Accounting Review, 70*(2), 337–353.

Billett, M. T., King, T. H. D., & Mauer, D. C. (2007). Growth opportunities and the choice of leverage, debt maturity, and covenants. *The Journal of Finance, 62*(2), 697–730.

Blaylock, B. S. (2016). Is tax avoidance associated with economically significant rent extraction among US firms? *Contemporary Accounting Research, 33*(3), 1013–1043.

Bradley, M., & Roberts, M. R. (2015). The structure and pricing of corporate debt covenants. *The Quarterly Journal of Finance, 5*(02), 1550001.

Brondolo, J. (2009). *Collecting taxes during an economic crisis: Challenges and policy options.* IMF Staff Position Notes 2009(017).

Butt, U. (2019). Debt covenant violation, competition and cost of new debt. *Australian Journal of Management, 44*(2), 163–187.

Chang, X., Dasgupta, S., Wong, G., & Yao, J. (2014). Cash-flow sensitivities and the allocation of internal cash flow. *The Review of Financial Studies, 27*(12), 3628–3657.

Charitou, A., Lambertides, N., & Trigeorgis, L. (2007). Earnings behaviour of financially distressed firms: The role of institutional ownership. *Abacus, 43*(3), 271–296.

Chava, S., & Roberts, M. R. (2008). How does financing impact investment? The role of debt covenants. *The Journal of Finance, 63*(5), 2085–2121.

Chen, K. P., & Chu, C. C. (2005). Internal control versus external manipulation: A model of corporate income tax evasion. *Rand Journal of Economics, 36*, 151–164.

Coase, R. H. (1937). The nature of the firm. *Economica, 4*(16), 386–405.

Crocker, K. J., & Slemrod, J. (2005). Corporate tax evasion with agency costs. *Journal of Public Economics, 89*(9), 1593–1610.

Daily, C. M., Dalton, D. R., & Rajagopalan, N. (2003). Governance through ownership: Centuries of practice, decades of research. *Academy of Management Journal, 46*(2), 151–158.

De Vito, A., & Jacob, M. (2021, November 27). The role of creditor protection in lending and tax avoidance. *Journal of Financial and Quantitative Analysis*. Available at SSRN: https://ssrn.com/abstract=3727201 or https://doi.org/10.2139/ssrn.3727201

DeAngelo, H., DeAngelo, L., & Skinner, D. J. (1994). Accounting choice in troubled companies. *Journal of Accounting and Economics, 17*(1–2), 113–143.

DeAngelo, H., & Masulis, R. W. (1980). Leverage and Dividend Irrelevancy Under Corporate and Personal Taxation. *The Journal of Finance, 35*(2), 453–464.

DeFond, M. L., & Jiambalvo, J. (1994). Debt covenant violation and manipulation of accruals. *Journal of Accounting and Economics, 17*(1–2), 145–176.

Demerjian, P. R., & Owens, E. L. (2016). Measuring the probability of financial covenant violation in private debt contracts. *Journal of Accounting and Economics, 61*(2–3), 433–447.

Demiroglu, C., & James, C. M. (2010). The information content of bank loan covenants. *The Review of Financial Studies, 23*(10), 3700–3737.

Desai, M. A., & Dharmapala, D. (2006). Corporate tax avoidance and high-powered incentives. *Journal of Financial Economics, 79*(1), 145–179.

Desai, M. A., & Dharmapala, D. (2009). Corporate tax avoidance and firm value. *Review of Economics and Statistics, 91*(3), 537–546.

Desai, M. A., Dyck, A., & Zingales, L. (2007). Theft and taxes. *Journal of Financial Economics, 84*, 591–623.

Dhaliwal, D. S., Huang, S. X., Moser, W. J., & Pereira, R. (2011). *Corporate tax avoidance and the level and valuation of firm cash holdings*. In 2011 American Accounting Association Annual Meeting-Tax Concurrent Sessions.

Dhawan, A., Ma, L., & Kim, M. H. (2020). Effect of corporate tax avoidance activities on firm bankruptcy risk. *Journal of Contemporary Accounting and Economics, 16*(2), 100187.

Diamond, D. W. (1991). Monitoring and reputation: The choice between bank loans and directly placed debt. *Journal of Political Economy, 99*(4), 689–721.

Dichev, I. D., & Skinner, D. J. (2002). Large–sample evidence on the debt covenant hypothesis. *Journal of Accounting Research, 40*(4), 1091–1123.

Dyreng, S. D., Hillegeist, S. A., & Penalva, F. (2022). Earnings management to avoid debt covenant violations and future performance. *European Accounting Review, 31*(2), 311–343.

Easley, D., & O'Hara, M. (2004). Information and the cost of capital. *Journal of Finance, 59*(4), 1553–1583.

Easterbrook, F. H. (1984). Two agency-cost explanations of dividends. *The American Economic Review, 74*(4), 650–659.

Edwards, A., Schwab, C., & Shevlin, T. (2016). Financial constraints and cash tax savings. *The Accounting Review, 91*(3), 859–881.

Eisdorfer, A. (2008). Empirical evidence of risk shifting in financially distressed firms. *The Journal of Finance, 63*(2), 609–637.

Eisenhardt, K. M. (1989). Agency theory: An assessment and review. *The Academy of Management review, 14*(1), 57–74.

Fama, E. F., & Jensen, M. C. (1983). Separation of ownership and control. *The Journal of Law and Economics, 26*(2), 301–325.

Flannery, M. J. (1986). Asymmetric information and risky debt maturity choice. *The Journal of Finance, 41*(1), 19–37.

Follett, M. P. (1924). *Creative experience.* Peter Smith.

Franz, D. R., HassabElnaby, H. R., & Lobo, G. J. (2014). Impact of proximity to debt covenant violation on earnings management. *Review of Accounting Studies, 19*, 473–505.

Freudenberg, F., Imbierowicz, B., Saunders, A., & Steffen, S. (2017). Covenant violations and dynamic loan contracting. *Journal of Corporate Finance, 45*, 540–565.

Galai, D., & Masulis, R. W. (1976). The option pricing model and the risk factor of stock. *Journal of Financial Economics, 3*(1–2), 53–81.

Gao, Y., Khan, M., & Tan, L. (2017). Further evidence on consequences of debt covenant violations. *Contemporary Accounting Research, 34*(3), 1489–1521.

Goh, B. W., Lee, J., Lim, C. Y., & Shevlin, T. (2016). The effect of corporate tax avoidance on the cost of equity. *The Accounting Review, 91*(6), 1647–1670.

Graham, J. R. (1996). Debt and the marginal tax rate. *Journal of Financial Economics, 41*(1), 41–73.

Graham, J. R. (2000). How big are the tax benefits of debt? *Journal of Finance, 55*, 1901–1942.

Graham, J. R. (2003). Taxes and corporate finance: A review. *The Review of Financial Studies, 16*(4), 1075–1129.

Graham, J. R., Lang, M. H., & Shackelford, D. A. (2004). Employee stock options, corporate taxes, and debt policy. *The Journal of Finance, 59*(4), 1585–1618.

Graham, J. R., & Tucker, A. L. (2006). Tax shelters and corporate debt policy. *Journal of Financial Economics, 81*, 563–594.

Green, D. H., & Kerr, J. N. (2022). How do firms use cash tax savings? A cross-country analysis. *Journal of the American Taxation Association, 44*(1), 93–121.

Guenther, D. A., Njoroge, K., & Williams, B. M. (2020). Allocation of internal cash flow when firms pay less tax. *The Accounting review, 95*(5), 185–210.

Habib, A., Costa, M. D., Huang, H. J., Bhuiyan, M. B. U., & Sun, L. (2020). Determinants and consequences of financial distress: Review of the empirical literature. *Accounting and Finance, 60*, 1023–1075.

Hanlon, M., & Heitzman, S. (2010). A review of tax research. *Journal of Accounting and Economics, 50*(2–3), 127–178.

Harris, M., & Raviv, A. (1988). Corporate control contests and capital structure. *Journal of Financial Economics, 20*, 55–86.

Harris, M., & Raviv, A. (1991). The theory of capital structure. *The Journal of Finance, 46*(1), 297–355.

Harvey, C. R., Lins, K. V., & Roper, A. H. (2004). The effect of capital structure when expected agency costs are extreme. *Journal of Financial Economics, 74*(1), 3–30.

Hasan, I., Hoi, C. K. S., Wu, Q., & Zhang, H. (2014). Beauty is in the eye of the beholder: The effect of corporate tax avoidance on the cost of bank loans. *Journal of Financial Economics, 113*(1), 109–130.

Hasan, M. M., Al-Hadi, A., Taylor, G., & Richardson, G. (2017). Does a firm's life cycle explain its propensity to engage in corporate tax avoidance?. *European Accounting Review, 26*(3), 469–501. https://doi.org/10.1080/09638180.2016.1194220

Hasan, M. M., Lobo, G. J., & Qiu, B. (2021). Organizational capital, corporate tax avoidance, and firm value. *Journal of Corporate Finance, 70*, 102050.

Heitzman, S. M., & Lester, R. (2021). Net operating loss carryforwards and corporate savings policies. *The Accounting Review.* https://doi.org/10.2308/TAR-2019-0085

Hill, C. W., & Jones, T. M. (1992). Stakeholder-agency theory. *Journal of Management Studies, 29*(2), 131–154.

Hoopes, J. L., Mescall, D., & Pittman, J. A. (2012). Do IRS audits deter corporate tax avoidance? *The Accounting Review, 87*(5), 1603–1639.

Huang, H. H., Lobo, G. J., Wang, C., & Xie, H. (2016). Customer concentration and corporate tax avoidance. *Journal of Banking and Finance, 72*, 184–200.

Jaggi, B., & Gul, F. A. (1999). An analysis of joint effects of investment opportunity set, free cash flows and size on corporate debt policy. *Review of Quantitative Finance and Accounting, 12*(4), 371–381.

Jensen, M. C. (1986). Agency costs of free cash flow, corporate finance, and takeovers. *The American Economic Review, 76*, 323–329. https://doi.org/10.2139/ssrn.99580

Jensen, M. C. (1988). Takeovers: Their causes and consequences. *Journal of Economic Perspectives, 2*(1), 21–48.

Jensen, M. C. (1989). Active investors, LBOs, and the privatization of bankruptcy. *Journal of Applied Corporate Finance, 2*(1), 35–44.

Jensen, M. C., & Meckling, W. H. (1976). Theory of the firm: Managerial behavior, agency costs and ownership structure. *Journal of Financial Economics, 3*(4), 305–360.

Jensen, M., & Roeback, R. (1983). The market for corporate control: Empirical evidence. *Journal of Financial Economics, 11*, 5–50.

Kaplan, S. E., & Ruland, R. G. (1991). Positive theory, rationality and accounting regulation. *Critical Perspectives on Accounting, 2*(4), 361–374.

Khurana, I. K., Moser, W. J., & Raman, K. K. (2018). Tax avoidance, managerial ability, and investment efficiency. *Abacus, 54*(4), 547–575.

Kim, J. B., Li, O. Z., & Li, Y. (2010). *Corporate tax avoidance and bank loan contracting.* Available at SSRN 1596209.

Kim, J. B., Li, Y., & Zhang, L. (2011). Corporate tax avoidance and stock price crash risk: Firm-level analysis. *Journal of Financial Economics, 100*(3), 639–662.

Kothari, S. P., Leone, A. J., & Wasley, C. E. (2005). Performance matched discretionary accrual measures. *Journal of Accounting and Economics, 39*(1), 163–197.

Lambert, R., Leuz, C., & Verrecchia, R. E. (2007). Accounting information, disclosure, and the cost of capital. *Journal of Accounting Research, 45*(2), 385–420.

Lasfer, M. A. (1995). Agency costs, taxes and debt: The UK evidence. *European Financial Management, 1*(3), 265–285.

Law, K. K., & Mills, L. F. (2015). Taxes and financial constraints: Evidence from linguistic cues. *Journal of Accounting Research, 53*(4), 777–819.

Lee, Y., Shevlin, T. J., & Venkat, A. (2022). The effect of tax avoidance on capital structure choices. *Journal of American Taxation Association.* https://doi.org/10.2308/JATA-19-049

Leland, H. E. (1998). Agency costs, risk management, and capital structure. *The Journal of Finance, 53*(4), 1213–1243.

Leland, H. E., & Pyle, D. H. (1977). Informational asymmetries, financial structure, and financial intermediation. *The Journal of Finance, 32*(2), 371–387.

Lim, Y. (2011a). Tax avoidance and underleverage puzzle: Korean evidence. *Review of Quantitative Finance and Accounting, 39*(3), 333–360.

Lim, Y. (2011b). Tax avoidance, cost of debt and shareholder activism: Evidence from Korea. *Journal of Banking and Finance, 35*(2), 456–470.

Lin, S., Tong, N., & Tucker, A. L. (2014). Corporate tax aggression and debt. *Journal of Banking and Finance, 40*, 227–241.

MacKie-Mason, J. K. (1990). Do taxes affect corporate financing decisions? *Journal of Finance, 45*, 1471–1493.

Maksimovic, V., & Zechner, J. (1991). Debt, agency costs, and industry equilibrium. *The Journal of Finance, 46*(5), 1619–1643.

Malitz, I. (1986). On financial contracting: The determinants of bond covenants. *Financial Management, 15*, 18–25.

Merton, R. K. (1940). Bureaucratic structure and personality. *Social Forces, 18*, 560–568.

Mills, L., & Newberry, K. (2001). The influence of tax and non-tax costs on book-tax reporting differences: Public and private firms. *Journal of the American Taxation Association, 23*(1), 1–19.

Morellec, E. (2004). Can managerial discretion explain observed leverage ratios? *The Review of Financial Studies, 17*(1), 257–294.

Mossin, J. (1968). Optimal multiperiod portfolio policies. *The Journal of Business, 41*(2), 215–229.

Myers, S. C. (1977). Determinants of corporate borrowing. *Journal of Financial Economics, 5*(2), 147–175.

Nini, G., Smith, D. C., & Sufi, A. (2012). Creditor control rights, corporate governance, and firm value. *The Review of Financial Studies, 25*(6), 1713–1761.

Noga, T. J., & Schnader, A. L. (2013). Book-tax differences as an indicator of financial distress. *Accounting Horizons, 27*(3), 469–489.

Ozelge, S., & Saunders, A. (2012). The role of lending banks in forced CEO turnovers. *Journal of Money, Credit and Banking, 44*(4), 631–659.

Panda, B., & Leepsa, N. M. (2017). Agency theory: Review of theory and evidence on problems and perspectives. *Indian Journal of Corporate Governance, 10*(1), 74–95.

Penman, S. H., & Penman, S. H. (2010). *Financial statement analysis and security valuation.* McGraw-Hill/Irwin.

Perrow, C. (1986). *Complex organizations.* Random House.

Phillips, J. D. (2003). Corporate tax-planning effectiveness: The role of compensation-based incentives. *The Accounting Review, 78*(3), 847–874.

Platikanova, P. (2017). Debt maturity and tax avoidance. *European Accounting Review, 26*(1), 97–124.

Rajan, R., & Winton, A. (1995). Covenants and collateral as incentives to monitor. *The Journal of Finance, 50*(4), 1113–1146.

Rajan, R. G., & Zingales, L. (1995). What do we know about capital structure? Some evidence from international data. *The Journal of Finance, 50*(5), 1421–1460.

Reisel, N. (2014). On the value of restrictive covenants: Empirical investigation of public bond issues. *Journal of Corporate Finance, 27*, 251–268.

Richardson, S. (2006). Over-investment of free cash flow. *Review of Accounting Studies, 11*(2–3), 159–189.

Richardson, G., Taylor, G., & Lanis, R. (2015). The impact of financial distress on corporate tax avoidance spanning the global financial crisis: Evidence from Australia. *Economic Modelling, 44*, 44–53.

Roberts, J. (2005). *Agency theory, ethics and corporate governance.* In *Corporate governance: Does any size fit?* Emerald Group.

Roberts, M. R., & Sufi, A. (2009). Renegotiation of financial contracts: Evidence from private credit agreements. *Journal of Financial Economics, 93*(2), 159–184.

Rosner, R. L. (2003). Earnings manipulation in failing firms. *Contemporary Accounting Research, 20*(2), 361–408.

Ross, S. A. (1973). The economic theory of agency: The principal's problem. *The American Economic Review, 63*(2), 134–139.

Ross, S. A. (1977). The determination of financial structure: The incentive-signalling approach. *The Bell Journal of Economics, 8*, 23–40.

Roychowdhury, S. (2006). Earnings management through real activities manipulation. *Journal of Accounting and Economics, 42*(3), 335–370.

Shevlin, T., Urcan, O., & Vasvari, F. P. (2020). Corporate tax avoidance and debt costs. *Journal of the American Taxation Association, 42*(2), 117–143.

Shleifer, A., & Vishny, R. W. (1997). A survey of corporate governance. *Journal of Finance, 52*(2), 737–789.

Simon, H. A. (1965). *Administrative behavior* (Vol. 4). Free Press.

Slemrod, J. (2004). The economics of corporate tax selfishness. *National Tax Journal, 57*(4), 877–899.

Smith, A. (1776). *An inquiry into the nature and causes of the wealth of nations.* (Vol. 1) Printed for W. Strahan and T. Cadell.

Smith, C. W., Jr., & Warner, J. B. (1979). On financial contracting: An analysis of bond covenants. *Journal of Financial Economics, 7*(2), 117–161.

Smith, C. W., Jr., & Watts, R. L. (1992). The investment opportunity set and corporate financing, dividend, and compensation policies. *Journal of Financial Economics, 32*(3), 263–292.

Stulz, R. (1988). Managerial control of voting rights: Financing policies and the market for corporate control. *Journal of Financial Economics, 20,* 25–54.

Tirole, J. (2006). *The theory of corporate finance.* Princeton University Press.

Trezevant, R. (1992). Debt financing and tax status: Tests of the substitution effect and the tax exhaustion hypothesis using firms' responses to the Economic Recovery Tax Act of 1981. *Journal of Finance, 47,* 1557–1568.

Tulkens, H., & Jacquemin, A. (1971). *The cost of delinquency: A problem of optimal allocation of private and public expenditure.* Katholieke Universiteit.

Vos, E., & Forlong, C. (1996). The agency advantage of debt over the lifecycle of the firm. *The Journal of Entrepreneurial Finance, 5*(3), 193–211.

Wagenhofer, A. (2015). *Agency theory: Usefulness and implications for financial accounting.* In *The Routledge companion to financial accounting theory* (pp. 361–385). Routledge.

Watts, R. L., & Zimmerman, J. L. (1986). *Positive accounting theory.* Prentice-Hall.

Weber, M. (1947). *The Theory of Social and Economic Organization.* Macmillan.

Wilson, R. (1968). The theory of syndicates. *Econometrica: Journal of the Econometric Society, 36,* 119–132.

Wilson, R. J. (2009). An examination of corporate tax shelter participants. *The Accounting Review, 84*(3), 969–999.

Chapter 4
Tax Avoidance and Debt Covenant Violation Across the Life Cycle Stages of a Firm

Keywords Tax avoidance · Debt covenant violation · Corporate life cycle · Free cash flow

4.1 Corporate Life Cycle: An Agency View

Originating from management and organization studies (e.g., Greiner, 1972; Gort & Klepper, 1982; Miller & Friesen, 1984), the corporate life cycle theory has recently gained considerable attention also in the accounting and finance literature [see Habib and Hasan (2019) for a review].

According to the lifecycle theory, firms follow a specific development trajectory over time, exhibiting different characteristics in terms of management style, resource planning and financial needs (Miller & Friesen, 1984; Dickinson, 2011). Prior literature indicates that increases of the cost-of-capital and of the undesired exacerbation of the firm's risk of default may occur at each point of a firm's lifespan (Koh et al., 2015; Kücher et al., 2020; Vurro et al., 2022). Yet, their causes and the likelihood to occur change across the various phases, as the result of a different commitment and discretion by the management the use of corporate resources available (Sirmon et al., 2011; Jensen, 1986).

Dickinson (2011) argued that the life cycle stage of a firm is not dependent on the firms' age, but rather on its cash-flow patterns. Cash flow patterns have a strong association with the firm's life cycle fundamentals and can explaining why, despite their age, firms may proceed across different, and often non-monotonically, development trajectories (Dickinson, 2011; Josefy et al., 2017).

Management scholars have specifically revealed the existence of five key and clearly predictable stages of the firms' evolution, namely: the introduction, the growth, the mature, the shake-out and decline stages (Gort & Klepper, 1982; Miller & Friesen, 1984). Each stage is featured by a specific cash flow pattern, different prosects of growth, and with by a distinctive degree of alignment of interests between the managers and the shareholders, which can determine, in turn, a higher (lower) managers' discretion in the employment of corporate resources (Dickinson, 2011; Jensen, 1986). Building on the Agency Theory and on the corporate life cycle theory, Filatotchev et al. (2006) and O'Connor and Byrne (2015) provided a theoretical framework that interprets the level of principal-agent interests' alignment as a complex relationship whose dynamic is featured by the stages of the corporate life cycle. Vos and Forlong (1996) add to this picture the changing role of the agency benefit of debt across the stages of the life cycle of a firm. They show that debt is expected to reach its optimum in terms of mitigation of agency conflicts between the shareholders and the managers (i.e., the debt monitoring hypothesis) when the firm enters the mature stage. Conversely, for firms in their early stages of the corporate life cycle, such as the introduction stage, debt financing have limited agency benefits and can, on the contrary, be associated to an exacerbation of existing financial distress and bankruptcy costs.

In the following paragraph, building on a theoretical agency framework of the corporate life cycle (Jensen, 1986; Dickinson, 2011; Vos & Forlong, 1996; Filatotchev et al., 2006; O'Connor & Byrne, 2015), I attempt a reconciliation of the two prior "views" regarding corporate tax avoidance and capital structure (i.e., the "tunneling view" and the "value-enhancing view"), by focusing on debt covenant as a critical feature of the firms' capital structure management.

4.2   Tax Avoidance and Debt Covenant Violation: A Theoretical Agency Framework Based on the Corporate Life Cycle

In the previous paragraph, I discussed prior literature examining the implications of tax avoidance for a firm's cost of capital and its related risk of default. Then, I focused on the debt covenant violation as a trigger of the firm's increases in the cost of capital and as a prominent early warning signal of the firm's risk of default (Beaver et al., 2011; Habib et al., 2020). In this paragraph, building on the Agency Theory and on the corporate life cycle theory (Jensen, 1986; Dickinson, 2011; Vos & Forlong, 1996; Filatotchev et al., 2006; O'Connor & Byrne, 2015), I explore the concept of corporate life cycle stage as a construct through which to reconcile, at least in part, the two competing predictions on the association between tax avoidance, debt covenant violation, and the related risk of financial default emerged from prior literature.

As previously anticipated, recent life cycle scholarship posits that each phase of a firm's lifespan is featured by a specific cash flow pattern, by distinct growth perspectives, and by a different degree of alignment of interests between the managers and the shareholders, which can determine, in turn, a higher (lower) managers' commitment (discretion) in the employment of corporate resources (e.g., Owen & Yawson, 2010; Dickinson, 2011; O'Connor & Byrne, 2015). According to Jensen (1986), cash flow patterns, as displayed by the level of free cash flow available, can signal the presence of higher or lower agency conflicts (Jensen, 1986). Hence, agency conflicts agency conflicts are expected to change across the life cycle stages of a firm (Habib & Hasan, 2019).

A first line of the literature (i.e., the "*value enhancing*" view), as discussed in details in Chap. 4, supports the thesis that tax avoidance is a benign activity, and that tax avoidance does not increase a firm's default risk, nor the possibility of rent extraction and that it is positively related with a firm's quality of the internal information environment and organizational capital (Gallemore & Labro, 2015; Blaylock, 2016; Guenther et al., 2017; Isin, 2018; Hasan et al., 2021). In line with this view, Robinson et al. (2010) show that firms benefit of lower tax rates when their tax department is evaluated as a profit center, rather than a cost center. Hence, tax avoidance can be used by firms as a value-increasing activity by managers and shareholders may purposely incentivize managers to pursue efficient tax minimization strategies [e.g., by structuring after-tax compensation contracts, see: Phillips (2003)]. If tax avoidance is an activity that could create value for firm and its shareholders, then, according to this view, engagement in corporate tax avoidance activities is more likely in context with limited shareholders-managers conflicts and where the marginal agency costs of debt (including, e.g., the cost of financial distress) prevail on the related marginal benefits (Hasan et al., 2017; Vos & Forlong, 1996). In such a context, cash resources from tax avoidance activities may not incur the risk to be hijacked by managers towards negative present value projects and are likely to be used by the managers to support value-increasing activities such as, repayment of firms' debt positions, reduction of excessive indebtment (and of its related costs), payout of cash dividends to shareholders, creation of precautionary cash holdings, and reconfiguration of an optimal capital structure (Guenther et al., 2020).

The life cycle theory predicts that agency conflicts between the managers and shareholders is absent or limited in the introduction and decline stage of a firm's life cycle, as these phases are typically featured by limited separation of ownership and control structure, limited or negative free cash flow available and by tightened constraints in the resources' uses and allocation by the managers (Filatotchev et al., 2006; Dickinson, 2011; Hasan et al., 2017). The expected marginal agency benefit from debt financing is also limited in these stages, as debt is unlikely to exert monitoring externalities on the management (Vos & Forlong, 1996). Tax benefits related to debt are also difficult to exploit in these phases, due to limited profitability and negative taxable income (Graham, 2003). Hence, introduction and decline stage firms are more likely than others to search and exploit sources of advantageous tax alternative to debt financing, which can span from benign deduction from tax losses to more aggressive forms of non-debt tax shields (e.g., tax avoidance and tax sheltering) (DeAngelo & Masulis, 1980; Hasan et al., 2017; De Vito & Jacob, 2021). Prior research suggests that, owing to limited conflicts between the managers and the shareholders on free cash flow available and to high financial distress costs related to debt financing, the exploitation of non-debt tax shields can become a prominent alternative source of financing (Jensen, 1986; DeAngelo & Masulis, 1980; Dickinson, 2011). In these stages, thus, tax avoidance likely increases the level of after-tax cash flow available and be negatively associated with debt covenant violation and to the related risk of financial default.

On the other hand, a second line of the tax literature (i.e., the *"tunneling"* view) indicates that tax avoidance is not a simple transfer of resources from a non-shareholder stakeholder (i.e., the State) to the firm's shareholder, because of agency conflicts afflicting the relationship between the managers and the shareholders (e.g., Desai et al., 2007; Desai & Dharmapala, 2006, 2009; Lim, 2011).[1] At a first, the substitution of debt with tax avoidance could reduce the risk of debt covenant violation, and the associated default risk, by increasing cash flow and diminishing the expected costs of bankruptcy associated with leverage financing (Kim et al., 2010; Graham & Tucker, 2006; Lim, 2011; Lin et al., 2014).[2] However, owing to the additive effect of tax avoidance on the firm's free cash flows, the potential benefit related to the debt reduction (i.e., reduction of expected bankruptcy costs) could be offset by an exacerbation of agency conflicts (Jensen, 1986; Desai et al., 2007; Desai & Dharmapala, 2009). Specifically, as the level of free cash flow increases—due to more tax avoidance—and the level of debt decreases due to the substitution effect, the bondholder's monitoring power over the firms' managers (and shareholders) weakens (Jensen, 1986). As a result, a higher level of tax avoidance could increase the portion of free cash flow that is available to managers for discretionary spending. Therefore, according to a "tunneling" view of tax avoidance—in context of high shareholders-managers agency conflicts and still unexploited marginal agency benefits of debt—a higher level of tax avoidance could increase the likelihood of debt covenant violation, and the associated default risk, owing to potential rent diversion, managerial entrenchment, and sub-optimal allocation of cash tax savings related to tax avoidance (Desai et al., 2007; Chan et al., 2016).[3] Consistently with this view, some previous studies suggested that capital market participants interpret tax avoidance as a red flag of rent extraction, hoard of bad news by managers, and as a signal of increased corporate reputational risks (e.g., Kim et al., 2011; Hasan et al., 2014; Platikanova, 2017; Shevlin et al., 2020).[4] Investors and lenders may negatively perceive tax avoidance and penalizing the firm by imposing stringent debt contract contingencies. Overall, these underlying effects could make tax avoidance less valuable to reduce the likelihood of debt covenant violation, and the related default risk (Noga & Schnader, 2013; Dhawan et al., 2020).

---

[1] The "tunneling effect" is consistent with the also reported "risk effect" of tax avoidance (Hasan et al., 2014; Cen et al., 2017), although this one might not necessarily consider agency conflicts.

[2] As leverage increases, the tax advantage of debt eventually will be offset by increased cost of debt, reflecting the greater likelihood of financial distress. (Leland, 1994, p. 1213)

[3] While not specifically attributing this result to agency conflicts, Green and Kerr (2022) find that cash tax savings from tax avoidance are positively associated with over-investment, but negatively associated to investment efficiency.

[4] Kim et al. (2011) provided evidence that equity-holders (i.e., *"residual claimants"*), although potentially beneficiaries of corporate tax avoidance, could interpret tax avoidance as a signal of agency problems and, thus, reacting to it by engaging in massive sales of the firm's stocks. Bondholders (i.e., *"fixed-claimants"*) do not expect to benefit from tax avoidance and, thus, they can react to it by increasing loan spreads and asking tax avoider firms for frequent renegotiation of debt contracts (Hasan et al., 2014; Platikanova, 2017).

The life cycle theory predicts that agency conflicts between the managers and shareholders on the free cash flow are stronger for firms in the mature stage of the corporate life cycle, as this phase is typically featured by a higher degree of separation between ownership and control, by the presence of larger available financial slack, and, overall, by a higher degree of opportunism by managers in the use and allocation of the corporate resources (Filatotchev et al., 2006; Dickinson, 2011; Hasan et al., 2017). In such a context, more than ever, the potential agency advantage from debt is at its most (Vos & Forlong, 1996; Habib & Hasan, 2019). Debt not only may provide firms with consistent tax advantages, due to a positive taxable income, but also positive monitoring externalities for the management (DeAngelo & Masulis, 1980; Jensen, 1986; Graham, 2003). Non-debt tax shields (e.g., tax avoidance and tax sheltering) are less likely to be an appealing source of financing for firms in this stage (DeAngelo & Masulis, 1980; Hasan et al., 2017; De Vito & Jacob, 2021). Hence, a higher level of tax avoidance in this stage is likely be related to managerial opportunism, harmful discretion, and potential wealth-extraction (Desai & Dharmapala, 2009). Investors and lenders may not expect tax avoidance from healthy and risk-adverse mature firms and can negatively react to them by imposing tightening debt contracting conditions, including more stringent covenants and collaterals (Kim et al., 2011; Hasan et al., 2014; Platikanova, 2017). Hence, in this stage, corporate tax avoidance activities are likely to negatively affect a firm's financial health, increasing the debt covenant violation likelihood and the related risk of financial default.

The argument offered, thus, is that the conflicting predictions from prior literature on the association between tax avoidance and debt covenant violation (i.e., the two "views") can be both valid and potentially reconcilable across the stages of a firm's life cycle, if the three endogenous mechanisms by which tax avoidance can affect the capital structure are jointly considered (i.e., the "free cash flow effect", the "debt substitution effect", "the debt monitoring effect"). Specifically, since tax avoidance is deemed to be an integral part of the firm's capital structure management (Richardson et al., 2015), any changes in the corporate tax status is accompanied by simultaneous changes in the firm's capital structure (e.g., the marginal benefit or cost expected from debt financing). The corporate life cycle stage, on the other hand, may influence the ex-ante level of agency conflicts between the shareholders and the managers, influencing the commitment of managers in the use of corporate resources, and, with it, the underlying motivations and aims of corporate tax avoidance activities.[5]

---

[5]The main assumption of this theoretical reconciliation is that life cycle-contingent cash flow patterns may convey, parsimoniously, relevant information on the underlying three main drivers affecting the tax avoidance-capital structure relationship, which are: (1) the level of free cash flow available and the related intensity Type I agency conflicts (i.e., the free cash flow effect); (2) the expected tax advantage from debt financing (i.e., the intensity of the debt-tax avoidance substitution); (3) the potential agency advantage of debt and the related intensity of Type II agency conflicts (i.e., debt monitoring hypothesis).

Directly, corporate tax avoidance impacts on the debt covenant violation likelihood and on the associated financial default risk since it modifies the firm's current and expected free cash flow. A higher free cash flow generating ability can reduce both priced and non-priced debt contracting conditions required by investors and lenders and ameliorate corporate financial conditions, reducing the debt covenant violation likelihood and the related risk of default. At the same time, however, a higher-level free cash flow can exacerbate existing agency conflicts between managers and shareholders on the use of corporate resources. Therefore, the benefit associated to the additional free cash flow can be offset by an increase in principal-agent agency costs.

Indirectly, tax avoidance impacts on debt covenant violation likelihood and on the related risk of financial default, since it re-balances the firm's debt and equity composition by lowering—*ceteris paribus* the firm's leverage posture (i.e., less sensitivity to the tax advantage of debt). At a first, a lower level of debt can be beneficial for the firm's financial health and being associated with a reduced risk of default. At the same time, however, in certain life cycle stages, a lower level of debt can exacerbate agency conflicts between managers and shareholders on the use of free cash flow. Therefore, the marginal benefit effect associated to the debt reduction can be offset by a reduction of the agency benefits of debt (i.e., rebounded increase of agency costs of free cash flow).[6] Basing on the free cash flow hypothesis and on the corporate life cycle theory, I formally stated the following theoretical propositions that relate the effect of corporate tax avoidance on the debt covenant violation likelihood.

Proposition 4.1 Ceteris paribus, *given the existence of a debt-tax avoidance substitution effect, tax avoidance is positively related to the likelihood of debt covenant violation in corporate life cycle stages featured by larger free cash flow and by marginal agency benefits of debt prevailing on the marginal agency costs of debt.*

Proposition 4.2 Ceteris paribus, *given the existence of a debt-tax avoidance substitution effect, tax avoidance is negatively related to the likelihood of debt covenant violation in corporate life cycle stages featured by absent or negative free cash flow and by marginal agency costs of debt prevailing on the marginal agency benefits of debt.*

In sum, it is suggested that the effect of tax avoidance on the default likelihood can vary depending on a firm's life cycle stage, as the result of a different ex-ante level of free cash flow and of its related agency conflicts.

---

[6]Under the Jensen's assumption that the marginal agency benefits of debt (i.e., debt monitoring hypothesis) outweigh its cost.

4.3 Tax Avoidance and Debt Covenant Violation: A Corporate Life Cycle Hypothesis

4.3.1 The Introduction Stage

In the introduction stage (also referred to as "start-up" stage), firms are young, simple, and unknown, and in need of resources for investments (Hasan et al., 2015; Dickinson, 2011; Jawahar & McLaughlin, 2001). Agency conflicts between shareholders and managers are "either absent or insignificant" in this phase (Certo et al., 2001). Most of the firms in this stage have a centralized organization structure (Miller & Friesen, 1984), with a limited separation of ownership and control (Fama & Jensen, 1983), and negative free cash flows from operations (Jensen, 1986; Dickinson, 2011). Tax avoidance of introduction firms mainly consists of legal tax minimization strategies (e.g., tax deferral strategies), consistent with the "loss framework" in which those firms operate (Jawahar & McLaughlin, 2001). These strategies have typically a limited likelihood to be challenged by tax authorities, and usually requires limited set-up costs (Hasan et al., 2017). Firms' operations and projects can be constrained by a lack of resources in this phase (Edwards et al., 2016; Hasan et al., 2017). As Watson (2015, p. 2) stated, *"taxes are an allocation of scarce resources to a non-shareholder stakeholder"*. Hence, cash tax payments can represent an undesired outflow which may threaten the firm's survival.

Both shareholders and managers may be willing to reduce tax expenses and expanding the level of financial resources available (Hasan et al., 2017). Thanks to little or absent agency conflicts between the managers and the shareholders, tax avoidance is likely to be use by managers of introduction firms as a resourcefulness tool, aimed at avoiding corporate financial risks. The survival of start-up firms is usually uncertain and their repayment prospects at risk (Zahra, 2021). Debt covenants are common in the bank loan agreements of introduction firms, featured by heavy losses and high financial volatility (Nikolaev, 2010; Oliveira & Monte-Mor, 2022). Owing to limited information asymmetries between the managers and the shareholders and a strong commitment in a shrewd use of firms' (limited) resources, cash savings from tax avoidance are likely to a useful source of financing for these firms, through which to repay financial debt and to support its competitive advantage creation process, consistent with a value-enhancing effect (Jensen, 1986; Desai & Dharmapala, 2009; Guenther et al., 2020). In the introduction stage, the marginal agency cost related to debt financing (including e.g., costs of financial distress) is likely to prevail on the agency benefit of debt (i.e., the debt monitoring function), owing to a limited separation between ownership and control and a negative free cash flow (Jensen, 1986; Vos & Forlong, 1996). Hence, tax avoidance is unlikely to be used as a rent-extracting tool by the managers in this phase. It is, thus, reasonable to expect that the generation of cash resources through tax avoidance may be useful to reduce firm's debt covenant violation likelihood in this stage. Thus, I formulate the following directional hypotheses:

HP1: *Tax avoidance is negatively associated with debt covenant violation in firms in the introductory stage of their life cycle.*

4.3.2 The Growth Stage

As firms enter the growth stage, the degree of separation between ownership and control becomes gradually more pronounced. In this stage, agency conflicts between managers and shareholders can be increasingly more intense, owing to concurrent processes of decentralization and functionalization (Fama & Jensen, 1983; Miller & Friesen, 1984; Dickinson, 2011).

Investors and lenders may not expect tax avoidance from growth firms and could perceive this activity as risky (Hasan et al., 2015, 2017). Owning to an increased product-market competition, projects experimentation, and increased investment needs, the risk of violating debt covenants can be still very likely for many firms in this stage (Oliveira & Monte-Mor, 2022). In the attempt to avoid or delay debt covenant violation, managers of growth firms may use tax avoidance as an additional source of financing. However, predicting whether higher tax avoidance is associated to higher or lower violation likelihood for firms in the growth stage is not trivial.

On the one hand, tax avoidance may provide growth firms with a cheaper alternative to debt financing especially when the investments needs cannot be satisfied with the operating cash flows, increasing the firm's repayment prospects and, thus, reducing the risk of covenants violation (Hasan et al., 2015; Barclay & Smith, 2005). On the other, cash resources retrieved from tax avoidance can incur the risk of be directed towards negative present value projects by the managers which can be detrimental for the interests of shareholders and of the lenders, increasing the risk of covenants violation (Dickinson, 2011; Filatotchev et al., 2006; Jensen, 1986). Since it is difficult to ex-ante predict whether growth firms would benefit or not from greater tax avoidance, I formulate the following unidirectional hypothesis:

HP2: *Tax avoidance is not associated with debt covenant violation in firms in the growth stage of their life cycle.*

4.3.3 The Mature Stage

As a firm's growth opportunities terminate, a firm enters the mature stage. In the mature stage, firms have generally a larger size and show typically a risk-adverse behavior, also thanks to a more stable environment in which they operate (Miller & Friesen, 1984; Easley, & O'Hara, 2004; Hasan et al., 2015). On average, mature firms should be less likely to incur a violation of debt covenants (Oliveira & Monte-Mor, 2022). Firms in the mature stage have high positive free cash flow (FCFs) available, because of a higher profitability, and a lower investment need compared to firms in other stages (Habib & Hasan, 2019; Faff et al., 2016). However, due to large FCFs disputed between the between managers and shareholders, agency conflicts are likely to be particularly strong for firms in this stage (Habib & Hasan, 2019).[7] Moreover, for firms in the mature stage, the marginal agency cost related to debt financing is likely to be lower than the related agency benefit (Vos & Forlong, 1996). Debt financing could exert a significant monitoring effect in this stage, disciplining managers towards a more accurate use of corporate resources both in the interests of the corporate shareholders and bondholders (Jensen, 1986; Vos & Forlong, 1996). Hence, in this stage, the use of tax avoidance as a source of financing is likely to exacerbate agency conflicts and to promote an opaque environment which can facilitate wealth expropriation and resource diversion by the managers (DeAngelo & Masulis, 1980; Desai et al., 2007). Both investors and lenders could perceive tax avoidance of mature stage firms as a potential source of risk (e.g., reputational risks) and adversely reacting to such activities (Kim et al., 2011; Hasan et al., 2014). Because cash resources from tax avoidance incur the risk of be hijacked by the managers towards negative present value activities that increase the variance of corporate cash flow, tax avoidance is likely to increase the risk of debt covenant violation in this stage. Hence, I formulate the following directional hypothesis:

HP3: *Tax avoidance is positively associated with debt covenant violation in firms in the mature stage of their life cycle.*

4.3.4 The Decline Stage

A firm's corporate lifespan ends with the decline stage, in which growth rates, cash flows from operations, and investments plunge (Hasan et al., 2017). In this stage, firm's survival is a primary concern for managers (and the shareholders) (Dickinson, 2011). In order to survive, managers of declining firms are required to take several responsive actions aimed at turning the firm around (Koh et al., 2015). These actions can take both the form of operational and financial restructuring aimed at providing resources to continue to operate as a going concern and preserving key relationships with the lenders and the suppliers (Dickinson, 2011; Koh et al., 2015; Richardson et al., 2015). Agency conflicts on free cash flows are likely to be low in declining firms, since both operating and investing activities cash flow are negative in this stage (Jensen, 1986; Dickinson, 2011). Additionally, in this stage, the marginal agency cost related to debt financing is likely to outweigh the related benefit (Jensen, 1986; Vos & Forlong, 1996). In a context of limited agency shareholders-managers conflicts and of limited agency benefits from debt, tax avoidance is likely to be used

---

[7]Mature-stage firms are plagued with higher agency problems (e.g., agency problems emanating from free cash flows) and, hence, are required to provide more disclosures to increase information transparency and reduce agency costs. (Habib & Hasan, 2019, p. 192)

Table 4.1 Graphical representation of the research hypotheses

Summary				
LIFE CYCLE STAGE	INTRODUCTION	GROWTH	MATURE	DECLINE
TYPE II AGENCY CONFLICTS				
Agency benefit of debt	Negative	Positive or Negative	Positive	Negative
Agency cost of debt	High	High or Low	Low	High
TYPE I AGENCY CONFLICTS				
Principal-Agent Agency Cost	Limited	Increasingly Higher	High	Increasingly Lower
Tax Benefits of Debt	Low	High or Low	High	Low
Probable consideration in using tax avoidance	**Reduce the risk of violation (HP1)**	**Reduce or increase the risk of violation (HP2)**	**Increase the risk of violation (HP3)**	**Reduce the risk of violation (HP4)**

as an alternative value-increasing source of financing, potentially benefitting both the shareholders and the lenders (Koh et al., 2015; Hasan et al., 2017). With financial constraints threatening firm's survival, cash resources freed up by tax avoidance activities are likely to be shrewdly used by managers to satisfy debt repayment needs and to meet bondholders' covenants requirements. Tax avoidance may act as a credit quality enhancing tool for firms in this phase, reducing the likelihood of debt covenant violation (Kim et al., 2010). Thus, it is reasonable to expect that tax avoidance has a negative association with debt covenant violation in the decline stage. I formulate the following directional hypothesis:

HP4: *Tax avoidance is negatively associated with debt covenant violation in firms in the decline stage of their life cycle.*

Here below, I provide a graphical representation of the research hypotheses (see Table 4.1).

References

Barclay, M., & Smith, C. (2005). The capital structure puzzle: The evidence revisited. *Journal of Applied Corporate Finance, 1*(1), 817.
Beaver, W. H., Correia, M., & McNichols, M. F. (2011). Financial statement analysis and the prediction of financial distress. *Foundations and Trends® in Accounting, 5*(2), 99–173.
Blaylock, B. S. (2016). Is tax avoidance associated with economically significant rent extraction among US firms? *Contemporary Accounting Research, 33*(3), 1013–1043. https://doi.org/10.1111/1911-3846.12174

Cen, W., Tong, N., & Sun, Y. (2017). Tax avoidance and cost of debt: Evidence from a natural experiment in China. *Accounting and Finance, 57*(5), 1517–1556. https://doi.org/10.1111/acfi.12328

Certo, T. S., Covin, J. G., Daily, C. M., & Dalton, D. R. (2001). Wealth and the effects of founder management among IPO-stage new ventures. *Strategic Management Journal, 22*, 641–658.

Chan, K. H., Mo, P. L. L., & Tang, T. (2016). Tax avoidance and tunneling: Empirical analysis from an agency perspective. *Journal of International Accounting Research, 15*(3), 49–66.

De Vito, A., & Jacob, M. (2021, November 27). The role of creditor protection in lending and tax avoidance. *Journal of Financial and Quantitative Analysis.* Available at SSRN: https://ssrn.com/abstract=3727201 or https://doi.org/10.2139/ssrn.3727201

DeAngelo, H., & Masulis, R. W. (1980). Leverage and dividend irrelevancy under corporate and personal taxation. *The Journal of Finance, 35*(2), 453–464. https://doi.org/10.1111/j.1540-6261.1980.tb02176.x

Desai, M. A., & Dharmapala, D. (2006). Corporate tax avoidance and high-powered incentives. *Journal of Financial Economics, 79*(1), 145–179. https://doi.org/10.1016/j.jfineco.2005.02.002

Desai, M. A., & Dharmapala, D. (2009). Corporate tax avoidance and firm value. *Review of Economics and Statistics, 91*(3), 537–546. https://doi.org/10.1162/rest.91.3.537

Desai, M. A., Dyck, A., & Zingales, L. (2007). Theft and taxes. *Journal of Financial Economics, 84*, 591–623. https://doi.org/10.1016/j.jfineco.2006.05.005

Dhawan, A., Ma, L., & Kim, M. H. (2020). Effect of corporate tax avoidance activities on firm bankruptcy risk. *Journal of Contemporary Accounting and Economics, 16*(2), 100187. https://doi.org/10.1016/j.jcae.2020.100187

Dickinson, V. (2011). Cash flow patterns as a proxy for firm life cycle. *The Accounting Review, 86*(6), 1969–1994. https://doi.org/10.2308/accr-10130

Easley, D., & O'Hara, M. (2004). Information and the cost of capital. *Journal of Finance, 59*(4), 1553–1583. https://doi.org/10.1111/j.1540-6261.2004.00672.x

Edwards, A., Schwab, C., & Shevlin, T. (2016). Financial constraints and cash tax savings. *The Accounting Review, 91*(3), 859–881.

Faff, R., Kwok, W. C., Podolski, E. J., & Wong, G. (2016). Do corporate policies follow a life-cycle? *Journal of Banking and Finance, 69*, 95–107. https://doi.org/10.1016/j.jbankfin.2016.04.009

Fama, E., & Jensen, M. (1983). Separation of ownership and control. *Journal of Law and Economics, 26*, 301–326.

Filatotchev, I., Toms, S., & Wright, M. (2006). The firm's strategic dynamics and corporate governance lifecycle. *International Journal of Managerial Finance, 2*, 256–279. https://doi.org/10.1108/17439130610705481

Gallemore, J., & Labro, E. (2015). The importance of the internal information environment for tax avoidance. *Journal of Accounting and Economics, 60*(1), 149–167. https://doi.org/10.1016/j.jacceco.2014.09.005

Gort, M., & Klepper, S. (1982). Time paths in the diffusion of product innovations. *Economic Journal, 92*(367), 630–653. https://doi.org/10.2307/2232554

Graham, J. R. (2003). Taxes and corporate finance: A review. *The Review of Financial Studies, 16*(4), 1075–1129. https://doi.org/10.1093/rfs/hhg033

Graham, J. R., & Tucker, A. L. (2006). Tax shelters and corporate debt policy. *Journal of Financial Economics, 81*, 563–594. https://doi.org/10.1016/j.jfineco.2005.09.002

Green, D. H., & Kerr, J. N. (2022). How do firms use cash tax savings? A cross-country analysis. *Journal of the American Taxation Association, 44*(1), 93–121. https://doi.org/10.2308/JATA-19-027

Greiner, L. (1972). Evolution and revolution as organizations grow. *Harvard Business Review, 50*(4), 37–46.

Guenther, D. A., Matsunaga, S. R., & Williams, B. M. (2017). Is tax avoidance related to firm risk? *The Accounting Review, 92*(1), 115–136.

Guenther, D. A., Njoroge, K., & Williams, B. M. (2020). Allocation of internal cash flow when firms pay less tax. *The Accounting Review, 95*(5), 185–210.

Habib, A., Costa, M. D., Huang, H. J., Bhuiyan, M. B. U., & Sun, L. (2020). Determinants and consequences of financial distress: Review of the empirical literature. *Accounting and Finance, 60*, 1023–1075. https://doi.org/10.1111/acfi.12400

Habib, A., & Hasan, M. M. (2019). Corporate life cycle research in accounting, finance and corporate governance: A survey, and directions for future research. *International Review of Financial Analysis, 61*(C), 188–201.

Hasan, M. M., Al-Hadi, A., Taylor, G., & Richardson, G. (2017). Does a firm's life cycle explain Its propensity to engage in corporate tax avoidance? *European Accounting Review, 26*(3), 469–501. https://doi.org/10.1080/09638180.2016.1194220

Hasan, I., Hoi, C. K. S., Wu, Q., & Zhang, H. (2014). Beauty is in the eye of the beholder: The effect of corporate tax avoidance on the cost of bank loans. *Journal of Financial Economics, 113*(1), 109–130. https://doi.org/10.1016/j.jfineco.2014.03.004

Hasan, M. M., Hossain, M., Cheung, A. W. K., & Habib, A. (2015). Corporate life cycle and cost of equity capital. *Journal of Contemporary Accounting and Economics, 11*(1), 46–60. https://doi.org/10.1016/j.jcae.2014.12.002

Hasan, M. M., Lobo, G. J., & Qiu, B. (2021). Organizational capital, corporate tax avoidance, and firm value. *Journal of Corporate Finance, 70*, 102050. https://doi.org/10.1016/j.jcorpfin.2021.102050

Isin, A. A. (2018). Tax avoidance and cost of debt: The case for loan-specific risk mitigation and public debt financing. *Journal of Corporate Finance, 49*, 344–378. https://doi.org/10.1016/j.jcorpfin.2018.01.003

Jawahar, I. M., & McLaughlin, G. L. (2001). Toward a descriptive stakeholder theory: An organizational life cycle approach. *Academy of management review, 26*(3), 397–414.

Jensen, M. C. (1986). Agency costs of free cash flow, corporate finance, and takeovers. *The American Economic Review, 76*, 323–329. https://doi.org/10.2139/ssrn.99580

Josefy, M. A., Harrison, J. S., Sirmon, D. G., & Carnes, C. (2017). Living and dying: Synthesizing the literature on firm survival and failure across stages of development. *Academy of Management Annals, 11*(2), 770–799. https://doi.org/10.5465/annals.2015.0148

Kim, J.-B. Li, O. Z. & Li, Y. (2010) Corporate Tax Avoidance and Bank Loan Contracting. Working Paper. Available at SSRN: https://ssrn.com/abstract=1596209 or https://doi.org/10.2139/ssrn.1596209

Kim, J. B., Li, Y., & Zhang, L. (2011). Corporate tax avoidance and stock price crash risk: Firm-level analysis. *Journal of Financial Economics, 100*(3), 639–662. https://doi.org/10.1016/j.jfineco.2010.07.007

Koh, S., Durand, R. B., Dai, L., & Chang, M. (2015). Financial distress: Lifecycle and corporate restructuring. *Journal of Corporate Finance, 33*, 19–33. https://doi.org/10.1016/j.jcorpfin.2015.04.004

Kücher, A., Mayr, S., Mitter, C., Duller, C., & Feldbauer-Durstmüller, B. (2020). Firm age dynamics and causes of corporate bankruptcy: Age dependent explanations for business failure. *Review of Managerial Science, 14*, 633–661. https://doi.org/10.1007/s11846-018-0303-2

Leland, H. E. (1994). Corporate debt value, bond covenants, and optimal capital structure. *The Journal of Finance, 49*(4), 1213–1252. https://doi.org/10.1111/j.1540-6261.1994.tb02452.x

Lim, Y. (2011). Tax avoidance, cost of debt and shareholder activism: Evidence from Korea. *Journal of Banking and Finance, 35*(2), 456–470.

Lin, S., Tong, N., & Tucker, A. L. (2014). Corporate tax aggression and debt. *Journal of Banking and Finance, 40*, 227–241. https://doi.org/10.1016/j.jbankfin.2013.11.035

Miller, D., & Friesen, P. (1984). A longitudinal study of the corporate life cycle. *Management Science, 30*(10), 1161–1183. https://doi.org/10.1287/mnsc.30.10.1161

Nikolaev, V. V. (2010). Debt covenants and accounting conservatism. *Journal of Accounting Research, 48*(1), 137–176. https://doi.org/10.1111/j.1475-679X.2009.00359.x

Noga, T. J., & Schnader, A. L. (2013). Book-tax differences as an indicator of financial distress. *Accounting Horizons, 27*(3), 469–489. https://doi.org/10.2308/acch-50481

O'Connor, T., & Byrne, J. (2015). Governance and the corporate life-cycle. *International Journal of Managerial Finance, 11*(1), 23–43. https://doi.org/10.1108/IJMF-03-2013-0033

Oliveira, W. D. C. D., & Monte-Mor, D. S. (2022). The influence of the organizational life cycle on the violation of financial covenants. *Revista Brasileira de Gestão de Negócios, 24*, 708–722.

Owen, S., & Yawson, A. (2010). Corporate life cycle and M&A activity. *Journal of Banking and Finance, 34*(2), 427–440. https://doi.org/10.1016/j.jbankfin.2009.08.003

Phillips, J. D. (2003). Corporate tax-planning effectiveness: The role of compensation-based incentives. *The Accounting Review, 78*(3), 847–874. https://doi.org/10.2308/accr.2003.78.3.847

Platikanova, P. (2017). Debt maturity and tax avoidance. *European Accounting Review, 26*(1), 97–124.

Richardson, G., Taylor, G., & Lanis, R. (2015). The impact of financial distress on corporate tax avoidance spanning the global financial crisis: Evidence from Australia. *Economic Modelling, 44*, 44–53. https://doi.org/10.1016/j.econmod.2014.09.015

Robinson, J. R., Sikes, S. A., & Weaver, C. D. (2010). Performance measurement of corporate tax departments. *The Accounting Review, 85*(3), 1035–1064.

Shevlin, T., Urcan, O., & Vasvari, F. P. (2020). Corporate tax avoidance and debt costs. *Journal of the American Taxation Association, 42*(2), 117–143.

Sirmon, D. G., Hitt, M. A., Ireland, R. D., & Gilbert, B. A. (2011). Resource orchestration to create competitive advantage: Breadth, depth, and life cycle effects. *Journal of Management, 37*(5), 1390–1412. https://doi.org/10.1177/0149206310385695

Vos, E., & Forlong, C. (1996). The agency advantage of debt over the lifecycle of the firm. *The Journal of Entrepreneurial Finance, 5*(3), 193–211. https://doi.org/10.57229/2373-1761.1191

Vurro, C., Romito, S., & Benassi, M. (2022). Too good to say goodbye? Effect of stakeholder orientation on the survival of large firms. *Long Range Planning, 55*(5), 102161. https://doi.org/10.1016/j.lrp.2021.102161

Watson, L. (2015). Corporate social responsibility, tax avoidance, and earnings performance. *The Journal of the American Taxation Association, 37*(2), 1–21. https://doi.org/10.2308/atax-51022

Zahra, S. A. (2021). The resource-based view, resourcefulness, and resource management in startup firms: A proposed research agenda. *Journal of Management, 47*(7), 1841–1860. https://doi.org/10.1177/01492063211018505

Chapter 5
Tax Avoidance and Debt Covenant Violation: Does Corporate Life Cycle Matter?

Keywords Tax avoidance · Debt covenant violation · Life cycle stage · Cash flow patterns

5.1 Research Motivation

This Chapter provides an empirical examination of the association between tax avoidance and debt covenant violation as conditioned by the corporate life cycle. Debt covenants are binding clauses demanding the debtor to satisfy specific accounting-based requirements (e.g., a minimum level of interest coverage or a maximum Debt-to-EBITDA). In a bank loan agreement, debt covenants serve at mitigating the agency costs borne by the lender (Roberts & Sufi, 2009; Franz et al., 2014). Therefore, the violation of a debt covenant (a.k.a., "technical default") can be a costly event for the firm (i.e., borrower), as it allows the lenders to exercise its contractual rights (Dyreng et al., 2022). Extant research shows that firms may use accounting discretion (e.g., earnings management) with the aim to avoid or delay such costly events (Demerjian & Owens, 2016). Kim et al. (2010) is the first to investigate the association between tax avoidance and debt covenant violation likelihood, suggesting that tax avoidance can reduce the likelihood of a violation. However, Kim et al. (2010) do not consider the role of corporate life cycle stage as a potential moderator of such relationship. Life cycle stages have distinctive cash flow patterns and reflect specific shareholders-managers conflicts of interests (Jensen, 1986; Dickinson, 2011; Hasan et al., 2017). Therefore, whether and how tax avoidance affects a firm's debt covenant violation likelihood is likely to be contingent on a firm's life cycle stage.

Previous studies suggest that tax avoidance is positively associated with non-optimal debt management practices and potential diversion of corporate resources by the managers, thus increasing the risk of a technical default (e.g., Hasan et al., 2014; Dhawan et al., 2020). Conversely, other studies suggest that tax avoidance is not related to agency conflicts and that it can be beneficial to reduce the risk of debt covenant violation, owing to a potential increase in the firm's after-tax cash flow (e.g., Blaylock, 2016; Kim et al., 2010; Bayar et al., 2018). In this study, I attempt to reconcile these strands of literature, arguing that the level of

A. Gabrielli, *Tax Avoidance and Capital Structure*, SIDREA Series in Accounting and Business Administration, https://doi.org/10.1007/978-3-031-30980-9_5

agency conflicts associated to each stage of the corporate life cycle moderates the relationship between tax avoidance and debt covenant violation.

Life cycle studies suggest that firms develop organically across clearly identifiable and predictable phases, namely: introduction, growth, mature, shake-out, decline (Gort & Klepper, 1982; Miller & Friesen, 1984; Habib & Hasan, 2019). Firms' transition from one stage to another is linked to important changes in agency relations between shareholders and managers (Filatotchev et al., 2006; O'Connor & Byrne, 2015). Scholars suggest that agency conflicts on the free cash flow are more severe when firms are mature (O'Connor & Byrne, 2015, p. 26; Habib & Hasan, 2019). Conversely, agency conflicts on free cash flow are nearly irrelevant when firms are in the introduction and decline phase (DeAngelo et al., 2006). Recent studies indicate that a firms' transition along the stages of the corporate life cycle is not related to the firms' age but, rather, is function of the firms' cash-flow patterns (Dickinson, 2011; Habib & Hasan, 2019). Therefore, a cash flow-based classification of the firm's life cycle is useful to analyze agency conflicts because cash flow patterns can signal the presence of increased agency conflicts (Jensen, 1986; Dickinson, 2011).

In this research, I use the concept of corporate life cycle stage to analyze whether the association between tax avoidance and debt covenant violation varies in different agency settings, as framed by a firm's life cycle stages. According to the prior literature, so far, "much attention has been focused on the largest mature companies listed on a stock market, concentrating on the static theorizing of the principal-agent perspective" (Filatotchev et al., 2006, p. 257). As a result, very little is known about firms in agency settings different to maturity (Filatotchev et al., 2006; O'Connor & Byrne, 2015). To the best of the author's knowledge, no prior study has investigated the association between tax avoidance and debt covenant violation in the various stages of the corporate life cycle. This research argues that agency conflicts related to each stage of the corporate life cycle may moderate the association between tax avoidance and debt covenant violation.

5.2   Research Methodology

This empirical study addresses the abovementioned research gap by investigating a sample of U.S. public firms during the period 1989–2012. The research regresses measures of tax avoidance (i.e., CASH FLOW ETR and GAAP ETRVol) on a debt covenant violation dependent dummy variable (Beaver et al., 2010). The moderator variable of the analyses is represented by the corporate life cycle. Corporate life cycle is operationalized by using the Dickinson model, that employs firms' cash-flow patterns information to identify the different stages of the corporate life cycle (Dickinson, 2011). The research also adds as control variables a set of financial ratios taken from the Altman model (i.e., Altman, 1968), and found to be associated with the risk of default by previous research (e.g., Bellovary et al., 2007; Beaver et al., 2010; Beaver et al., 2018; Chava & Jarrow, 2004; Campbell et al., 2008).

To ensure that the analyses are not influenced by the impact of potential time-variant characteristics (e.g., macroeconomic trends, and year-specific regulation), the research runs the analyses using years-fixed effects. Moreover, the research adds industry-fixed effects to provide control over industry-specific characteristics, such as industry-specific tax law requirements (Heitzman & Ogneva, 2019), and industry-specific life cycle patterns (Agarwal & Audretsch, 2001; Drake & Martin, 2018). Standard errors clustered at a firm level are also included to control for firm-level fixed effects.

Following previous research on corporate life cycle (e.g., Owen & Yawson, 2010; Hasan et al., 2017), the paper develops the main analyses basing on a twofold approach. To start with, the study runs the main analyses by including the stages of the corporate life cycle together in the same model (i.e., *Pooled analysis*). Then, it re-runs the same analyses by incorporating stage-specific life cycle information one by one (i.e., *Life cycle-wise analyses*). To strengthen the results, the study also performs a battery of robustness checks and endogeneity tests (Wooldridge, 2002). Specifically, the study uses a propensity score matching analysis to identify a control sample of non-debt covenant violators with similar characteristics in term of size, performance, leverage and liquidity, industry and year. The remainder of this paragraph is organized as follows: Sect. 5.2.1. presents the description of the sample used for the analyses; Sect. 5.2.2. provides a description of the research design adopted. In this latter section, a detailed explanation of the variables used, and their measurement is also included.

5.2.1 Sample

The empirical analyses are based on a sample of U.S. public firms. The U.S. setting is of particular interest for the context of this examination for at least three main reasons. First, the U.S. debt market represents the largest, most reliable, and liquid market in the world (Quinn, 2019).[1] The use of debt covenants in debt agreements is a long-established practice within the U.S. (Beneish & Press, 1995; Taylor, 2013). Furthermore, U.S. public firms are subject to the SEC Regulation S-X (Rule 4-08(c)) and to US GAAP (ASC 470-10-45-1—11) which require disclosure of information pertaining to covenant violations. According to the Regulation S-X, firms are required to disclose facts and amount pertaining to any non-cured or waived obligation. The US GAAP completes the regulatory framework by requesting violating firms to classify the requirements for any obligations for which a covenant violation has been occurred.

Second, most of extant literature on debt covenant violation focused on the specific context of U.S. public firms [see Taylor (2013) for a review]. While future research on non-U.S. contexts is certainly to be encouraged, a relative advantage of

---

[1] see, also: https://cbonds.com/country/USA-bond/

examining a sample of U.S. firms is that of obtaining results that could directly map into prior literature, eliminating the possibility that potentially unobservable hetero-geneity related to country-specific institutional features may affect the results.

The sample's data are retrieved from the Compustat North America database. Specifically, I downloaded financial statements data both for active and inactive US firms. Then, I merged these data with covenant violations data reported in the SEC filings, publicly provided by Prof. Michael Roberts, representing an updated and extended version of that one used in Roberts and Sufi (2009). The sample time frame starts in 1996, since this is the first year in which data on debt covenant violations for U.S. public firms have been collected. The sample time frame ends in 2012, as it represents the last year in which data on debt covenants violation are publicly available. The database used represents an authoritative source of data about debt covenant violation, easily accessible, and well established within the finance community (see e.g., Moore & Xu, 2018; Altman et al., 2019; Gam & Liu, 2022).

The initial sample comprises 193,125 firm-year observations during the 1996–2012 period. After excluding the firm-year observations without complete data, a final sample of 52,368 firm-year observations is obtained.

5.2.2 Research Design and Variables Measurements

To test the hypotheses, I run two different analyses. First, I run a pooled analysis by including all the stages of the corporate life cycle in the same model, defined as in Eq. (5.1).

Equation 5.1: Pooled Regression

$$
\begin{aligned}
\text{Violation}_{it} = {} & \beta_0 + \beta_1 (\text{Tax Avoidance})_{i,t-1} + \beta_2 (\text{Introduction})_{i,t} \\
& + \beta_3 (\text{Tax Avoidance})_{i,t-1} \times (\text{Introduction})_{i,t} + \beta_2 (\text{Growth})_{i,t} \\
& + \beta_3 (\text{Tax Avoidance})_{i,t-1} \times (\text{Growth})_{i,t} + \beta_4 (\text{Mature})_{i,t} \\
& + \beta_5 (\text{Tax Avoidance})_{i,t-1} \times (\text{Mature})_{i,t} + \beta_6 (\text{Decline})_{i,t} \\
& + \beta_6 (\text{Tax Avoidance})_{i,t-1} \times (\text{Decline})_{i,t} + \beta_7 (\text{WC\_TA})_{i,t-1} + \beta_8 (\text{RE\_TA})_{i,t-1} \\
& + \beta_9 (\text{Ebit\_TA})_{i,t-1} + \beta_{10} (\text{MV\_TL})_{i,t-1} + \beta_{11} (\text{S\_TA})_{i,t-1} \\
& + \sum_{t=0}^{n} \text{Year Fixed Effects} - \text{Industry Fixed Effects} + \varepsilon_{i,t}
\end{aligned}
$$

Second, I run our main model by developing specific regressions for each stage of the corporate life cycle (i.e., life cycle-wise analysis). Following Hasan et al., 2017 the aim of the life cycle-wise analysis is to ascertain whether each stage of the corporate life cycle explains the same variations in the financial default risk observed in the pooled regression, once having considered tax avoidance, the stage of the corporate life cycle, and the stage-specific level of tax avoidance, in addition to the other control variables. The life cycle-wise analysis is performed using the models defined as in Eq. (5.2).

Equation 5.2: Life Cycle-Wise Regressions

Introduction Stage

$$\text{Violation}_{it} = \beta_0 + \beta_1(\text{Tax Avoidance})_{i,t-1} + \beta_2(\text{Introduction})_{i,t}$$
$$+ \beta_3(\text{Tax Avoidance})_{i,t-1} \times (\text{Introduction})_{i,t} + \beta_4(\text{WC\_TA})_{i,t-1}$$
$$+ \beta_5(\text{RE\_TA})_{i,t-1} + \beta_6(\text{Ebit\_TA})_{i,t-1} + \beta_7(\text{MV\_TL})_{i,t-1} + \beta_8(\text{S\_TA})_{i,t-1}$$
$$+ \sum\nolimits_{t=0}^{n} \text{Year Fixed Effects} - \text{Industry Fixed Effects} + \varepsilon_{i,t}$$

Growth Stage

$$\text{Violation}_{it} = \beta_0 + \beta_1(\text{Tax Avoidance})_{i,t-1} + \beta_2(\text{Growth})_{i,t}$$
$$+ \beta_3(\text{Tax Avoidance})_{i,t-1} \times (\text{Growth})_{i,t} + \beta_4(\text{WC\_TA})_{i,t-1} + \beta_5(\text{RE\_TA})_{i,t-1}$$
$$+ \beta_6(\text{Ebit\_TA})_{i,t-1} + \beta_7(\text{MV\_TL})_{i,t-1} + \beta_8(\text{S\_TA})_{i,t-1}$$
$$+ \sum\nolimits_{t=0}^{n} \text{Year Fixed Effects} - \text{Industry Fixed Effects} + \varepsilon_{i,t}$$

Mature Stage

$$\text{Violation}_{it} = \beta_0 + \beta_1(\text{Tax Avoidance})_{i,t-1} + \beta_2(\text{Mature})_{i,t}$$
$$+ \beta_3(\text{Tax Avoidance})_{i,t-1} \times (\text{Mature})_{i,t} + \beta_4(\text{WC\_TA})_{i,t-1} + \beta_5(\text{RE\_TA})_{i,t-1}$$
$$+ \beta_6(\text{Ebit\_TA})_{i,t-1} + \beta_7(\text{MV\_TL})_{i,t-1} + \beta_8(\text{S\_TA})_{i,t-1}$$
$$+ \sum\nolimits_{t=0}^{n} \text{Year Fixed Effects} - \text{Industry Fixed Effects} + \varepsilon_{i,t}$$

Decline Stage

$$\text{Violation}_{it} = \beta_0 + \beta_1(\text{Tax Avoidance})_{i,t-1} + \beta_2(\text{Decline})_{i,t}$$
$$+ \beta_3(\text{Tax Avoidance})_{i,t-1} \times (\text{Decline})_{i,t} + \beta_4(\text{WC\_TA})_{i,t-1} + \beta_5(\text{RE\_TA})_{i,t-1}$$
$$+ \beta_6(\text{Ebit\_TA})_{i,t-1} + \beta_7(\text{MV\_TL})_{i,t-1} + \beta_8(\text{S\_TA})_{i,t-1}$$
$$+ \sum\nolimits_{t=0}^{n} \text{Year Fixed Effects} - \text{Industry Fixed Effects} + \varepsilon_{i,t}$$

Both the models are estimated through a hazard model. I use the hazard model since it allows to examine the probability that a firm will experience a default event like a debt covenant violation at each point in time (Shumway, 2001). As such, the hazard model is particularly suitable for our examination given the dynamic nature of default. In addition to the Hazard model, I also adopted a standard logit model. I employ the logit model since it represents the base model in studies examining debt covenant violation (e.g., Kim et al., 2010; Dyreng et al., 2022).

All the models developed include industry and year fixed effects, in addition to standard errors clustered at a firm level. Specifically, year-fixed effects are used to provide control over time-variant characteristics in the sample, such as changes in macro-economic trends and modifications in the regulatory and normative environment. Industry fixed effects provide control for industry-specific characteristics including industry-specific tax law requirements (Heitzman & Ogneva, 2019), and industry-specific life cycle patterns (Agarwal & Audretsch, 2001; Drake & Martin, 2018). Standard errors clustered by firms to alleviate systematic serial correlation as well as to control for firm-level fixed effects.

Dependent Variable: Debt Covenant Violation

I built a measure of debt covenant violation using covenant violations data reported in the SEC filings during the 1996–2012 for U.S. public firms. I merged these data with the Compustat sample. Then, I operationalized the dependent variable—debt covenant violation ($Violation_{it}$)—as a dummy variable taking value of 1 for each firm-year observation of a firm disclosing a debt covenant violation, and 0 otherwise.

Independent Explanatory Variables: Tax Avoidance

Tax Avoidance$_{i,\ t\ -\ 1}$ is the model's independent explanatory variable. Consistent with Hanlon and Heitzman (2010), I define tax avoidance as a broad range of tax payment reduction activities, which ranges from legal tax strategies compliant with the tax law (e.g., benign tax-advantaged investments) to most aggressive strategies with a higher likelihood of being disallowed upon audit by tax authorities (e.g.,, aggressive interpretation of ambiguous areas of tax law).[2] In developing analyses on debt covenant violation, I use the *Cash Flow* ETR as proxy for tax avoidance (Guenther et al., 2017). Guenther et al. (2017) demonstrate that a cash flow-based definition of the effective tax rate can capture tax avoidance that is not related with earnings management. Earnings management literature suggest that that debt covenant violation is often anticipated by intense upward accrual-based income manipulation, since income-based accounting ratios are commonly incorporated in debt contracts (Demerjian & Owens, 2016). Hence, the *Cash Flow* ETRs can be an appropriate proxy to capture tax avoidance unrelated to earnings management. I calculated the *Cash Flow* ETR as the ratio between cash taxes paid ("*txpd*") on operating cash flow ("*opcf*") net of extraordinary items ("*xi*") (see also: Zimmerman, 1983). I also measured tax avoidance using the long-term standard deviation of ETRs (i.e., GAAP ETR*Vol*). The GAAP ETR*Vol* is a measure of tax avoidance that captures the risk inherent in the corporate tax positions (e.g., Drake et al., 2019). Blouin (2014) suggests that the combination of effective tax rates with the volatility of effective tax rates can provide a truthful and more complete picture of the corporate tax avoidance and of its inherent level of risk. In developing all the models,

---

[2] See also Wang et al. (2020).

I used lagged independent explanatory variables. The use of lagged explanatory variables can help mitigating endogeneity concerns from reverse causality (Vergara, 2010). Therefore, using lagged explanatory variables could provide a more conservative examination setting over potential endogeneity bias. All the proxies used to measure tax avoidance are winsorized at 1 and 99% to avoid the impact of outliers. Basing on the extant literature, it is not possible to provide a conclusive expectation on the predicted sign for tax avoidance proxies. On the one hand, Kim et al. (2010), in its unpublished paper, state that tax avoidance is negatively associated to the debt covenant violation likelihood. However, Kim et al. (2010) use tax avoidance variables (i.e., standard GAAP ETR) that are more likely to be afflicted to earnings management considerations compared to the Cash Flow ETR variable used in this study. On the other hand, other studies suggest that tax avoidance is perceived by the lenders as a risky activity, thus increasing the probability of a debt covenant violation (e.g., Hasan et al., 2014; Platikanova, 2017).

Moderator Variable: Corporate Life Cycle

$Lifecycle_{i,\ t}$ is a dummy variable which identifies the firm's life cycle stage at the time the firm faced the default event (i.e., the violation of the debt covenant). As detailed described at Chap. 4, I expect that corporate life cycle modifies the association between tax avoidance and debt covenant violation. Specifically, I expect that in context with low agency conflicts between the shareholders and the managers (and high agency costs of debt), like the introduction and the decline stage, a higher level of tax avoidance (i.e., lower Cash Flow ETR or higher GAAP ETR Volatility) is associated to a lower debt covenant violation likelihood. Conversely, in context of high agency conflicts between shareholders and managers (and high agency advantage of debt), like the mature stage, tax avoidance is likely to be used to rent extraction and positively associated to financial reporting opacity, reputational risks, and higher uncertainty on the level of future cash flow, resulting in a higher debt covenant violation likelihood.[3]

Following prior studies (e.g., Drake, 2015; Koh et al., 2015; Hasan et al., 2017), I proxied the different phases of the corporate life cycle by using firms' cash-flow patterns as in Dickinson (2011). Specifically, I adopt the Dickinson model since it provides a more objective and less erroneous identification of corporate life cycle with respect to other classification criteria (see Habib & Hasan, 2019 for a review of life cycle measurements).[4] Basing on it, I defined the corporate life cycle stages as follows:

---

[3] Given the general difficulty in predicting outcomes for firms in the growth stage (see Black, 2003), I do not advance any expectations for firms in this stage of the corporate life cycle.

[4] I acknowledge the existence of alternative identification strategies for corporate life cycle. Alternative identification strategies include the life cycle-based portfolio categorization developed by Anthony and Ramesh (1992), and the methodology developed by DeAngelo et al. (2006), which uses the retained earnings on total assets (or total equity) ratio as a descriptor of the corporate life cycle. There is a general consensus in the literature that these methods are less effective or more erroneous than the Dickinson model in the identification of the different stages of corporate life cycle (Hasan et al., 2017, and Habib & Hasan, 2019 for a review). For example, the Anthony and

INTRODUCTION: if OANCF < 0, INVCF < 0, and FINCF > 0;
GROWTH: if OANCF > 0, IVNCF < 0, and FINCF > 0;
MATURE: if OANCF > 0, INVCF < 0, and FINCF < 0;
DECLINE: if OANCF < 0, INVCF > 0, and FINCF $< = $ or $= > 0$; and
SHAKE-OUT: the rest of firm-years not classified as introduction, growth, mature, or decline.

Given the residual nature of the shake-out stage, previous studies do not consider this stage in their analyses or included it only as a benchmark (Koh et al., 2015; Hasan et al., 2017). Accordingly, I do not consider the shake-out stage in our analyses.

Control Variables

The research entails as control variables a set of financial ratios excerpted from the Altman model (Altman, 1968). These ratios have been demonstrated to be associated with the default by numerous studies [Bellovary et al. (2007) for a review]. Hence, these ratios can provide a parsimonious set of controls over the firms' characteristics associated to debt covenant violation other than our independent explanatory variable. In addition to controlling for firm's characteristics associated to financial default, the use of the Altman model can also limit the discretion in the choice of control covariates.

Basing on Altman (1968), I add control for: Working Capital/Total Assets ("WC_TA"); Retained Earnings/Total Assets ("RE_TA"); Earnings before interest and taxes/Total Assets ("EBIT_TA"); market value/total liabilities ("MV_TL"); sales/total assets ("S_TA").

WC_TA is obtained as the difference between current assets and current liabilities divided for total assets. This variable is a measure of corporate liquidity, which denotes the level of net liquid assets on the total capital invested. Generally, firms with low liquidity would be more likely to experience financial distress (Muñoz-Izquierdo et al., 2020). However, a high level of WC_TA does not mean immune from experiencing debt covenant violation, especially if the higher level of working capital is the result of doubtful accounting receivables, including trade receivables, or of a high inventory storage (Molina & Preve, 2009, 2012; Zhang, 2019; Chod, 2017). RE_TA is a measure of cumulated profitability, implicitly related to the firms' age. On average, the RE_TA ratio increases as the firm becomes older. EBIT_TA is a measure of firm's profitability. Specifically, this ratio reflects the part of corporate

---

Ramesh method can be difficult to implement since it requires five-year history for each variable. Therefore, its adoption can also make difficult the interpretation of early stages of the corporate life cycle (i.e., the introduction stage). Another acknowledged caveat in employing the Anthony and Ramesh (1992) model relates to the use of the firm's age as a descriptor of the corporate life cycle. This descriptor can be problematic as it assumes that firms progress linearly along the stages of their corporate life cycle (Dickinson, 2011; Faff et al., 2016; Habib & Hasan, 2019). DeAngelo et al. (2006) model could be helpful to overcome such limitation. Nonetheless, this method could still be ineffective in correctly classifying firms into different life cycle stages (Habib & Hasan, 2019). Moreover, this methodology can be hardly feasible in our research since the Altman Model already control for retained earnings on total assets (RE_TA).

profitability that arises from the firm productivity at net of any leverage or tax effect. This control is important for our examination as it permits us to parse out the effect of tax avoidance on risk of debt covenant violation, while limiting the risk that negative corporate performance could affect the interpretation of our results. I, thus, expect a positive correlation between RE_TA and debt covenant violation (Altman, 1968).

MV_TL is a measure calculated as the sum of the market value of common and ordinary shares on the firms' total liabilities. The MV_TL ratio measures the market value of the firm's equity compared to its total liabilities. The higher is the nominator of the ratio, the lower should the firm's probability of default (Altman, 1968). Hence, shrinkage of this variable could signal potential financial difficulties (Muñoz-Izquierdo et al., 2020). It can thus be expected a negative association between the MV_TL ratio and the firm's probability of debt covenant violation, since violation is more likely in highly leverage distressed firms (Jaggi & Lee, 2002).

Finally, the S_TA (a.k.a, asset-turnover ratio) measures the total assets contribution to the firms' sales generating activities (Altman, 1968). Although firms more likely to experience covenant violation or financial distress should show a lower value of the S_TA ratio, scholars several scholars have suggested that S_TA may not be a good financial distress predictor as one could expect (Altman et al., 2019; Shumway, 2001). Hence, I do not advance ex-ante a specific expectation for the sign of this variable.

Again, all the financial ratios included in the bankruptcy prediction model and the proxies of tax avoidance used are winsorized at 1 and 99%, to avoid the presence of outliers. Table 5.1 provides a summary of the variables used in this study and their empirical operationalization.

5.3 Empirical Results

5.3.1 Descriptive Statistics

Table 5.2 displays the sample descriptive statistics for all the main variable included in the analyses during the period 1996–2012 and using debt covenant violation as dependent variable. The total number of firms that incurred a debt covenant violation during the sample timeframe is of 999 observations counting for the 1.9% of the total sample's firm-years observations (52,368). The total number of firms that has not incurred a debt covenant violation in the sample timeframe investigated is of 51,369, counting for the 98.1% of the total sample's firm-year observations.[5]

---

[5]When violation is equal to 1 for the firm-year observation in which the firm discloses a debt covenant violation. Note that descriptive statistics reported at Table 5.2 refers to the sample statistics at time t. However, in all the analyses I use 1-year lagged values of the reported variable to control for potential endogeneity from reverse causality (Vergara, 2010).

Table 5.1 Summary of the variables used, their measurement, and their source

Dependent variable	
Debt covenant violation	
Violation	Binary variable equals to 1 if a firm discloses the violation of a debt covenant in the year t, and 0 otherwise
	Source: the variable "Debt Covenant Violation" is built basing on firm-years observation concerning the violation of a debt covenant (Roberts & Sufi, 2009). These information are publicly available at the Prof. Michael Roberts personal website (http://finance.wharton.upenn.edu/~mrrobert/styled-9/styled-11/index.html)
Independent variables	
Tax avoidance	
GAAP ETR*Vol*	Calculated as five year (t, $t - 4$) standard deviation of GAAP ETR (e.g., Drake et al., 2019; Christensen et al., 2022).
	Source: "txt" and "pi" variables are retrieved from Compustat North America Database
Cash Flow ETR	Calculated as Cash taxes paid ("*txpd*") on operating cash flow ("*opcf*") net of extraordinary items ("*xi*") (Guenther et al., 2017)
	Source: "txpd", "opcf", and "xi" are retrieved from Compustat North America Datatbase
Moderator variable	
Life cycle (Dickinson, 2011)	
Introduction	Binary variable equals to 1 if the firm has negative cash flow from operating activities (OANCF < 0), negative cash flow from investing activities (INVCF < 0) and positive cash flow from financing activities (FINCF > 0).
	Source: items "oancf", "invcf" and "fincf" are retrieved from Compustat North American Database
Growth	Binary variable equals to 1 if the firm has positive cash flow from operating activities (OANCF > 0), negative cash flow from investing activities (IVNCF < 0) and positive cash flow from financing activities (FINCF > 0)
	Source: items "oancf", "invcf" and "fincf" are retrieved from Compustat North American Database
Mature	Binary variable equals to 1 if the firm has positive cash flow from operating activities (OANCF > 0), negative cash flow from investing activities (IVNCF < 0), and negative cash flow from financing activities (FINCF < 0).
	Source: items "oancf", "invcf" and "fincf" are retrieved from Compustat North American Database
Shake-out	Binary variable equals to 1 if a firm is not as a firm in the introduction, growth, mature or decline stage
	Source: items "oancf", "invcf" and "fincf" are retrieved from Compustat North American Database
Decline	Binary variable equals to 1 if the firm has negative cash flow from operating activities (OANCF < 0), positive cash flow from investing activities (IVNCF > 0) and negative or positive cash flow from financing activities (FINCF < 0 or FINCF>0).
	Source: items "oancf", "invcf" and "fincf" are retrieved from Compustat North American Database

(continued)

Table 5.1 (continued)

Dependent variable	
Control variables	
WC_TA	Calculated as Working Capital ("WC"), obtained as the difference of current assets and current liabilities (item: "wcap", equivalent to the difference between "act" and "lct"), divided by the firms' Total Assets (item "at") *Source*: items "wcap", "act", "lct" and "at" are retrieved from Compustat North America
RE_TA	Calculated as Retained Earnings (item "re") divided by Total Assets (item "at") *Source:* items "re" and "at" are retrieved from Compustat North America
EBIT_TA	Calculated as Earnings before Interest and Taxes (item "ebit") divided by Total Assets (item "at") *Source*: items "ebit" and "at" variables are retrieved from Compustat North America
MV_TL	Calculated as Market Value of Equity ("MV"), obtained by multiplying the firm's stock price at the fiscal year end (item "prcc_f") for the firm's common shares outstanding (item "csho"), divided by Total Liabilities (item "lt") *Source*: items "prcc_f", "csho", and "lt" are retrieved from Compustat North America
S_TA	Calculated as Sales (item "salepfc", corresponding to "Pro Forma Net Sales-Current Year) on Total Assets ("at") *Source*: "salepcf" and "at" are retrieved from Compustat North America

Explanatory and Control variables are winsorized at 1 and 99%

Table 5.2 reports the sample descriptive statistics for the subsample of the non-violator firms (i.e., dependent variable equals to zero); violator firms (i.e., dependent variable equals to one), and violator and non-violator firms together (i.e., Total).

The explanatory variable of this study is tax avoidance, proxied both Cash Flow ETR as well as GAAP ETR*Vol*. The mean Cash Flow ETR is equal to 0.227 (22.7%). Specifically, the mean Cash Flow ETR is equal to 0.241 (24.1%) for the subsample of non-violator firms and equal to 0.170 (17.0%) for the subsample of violator firms (i.e., firms which incurred into a covenant violation at time t). The mean value of the Cash Flow ETR is in line with the mean value provided by Guenther et al. (2017), which is equal to 0.206 (20.6%).[6] The descriptive evidence for the sub-groups of violator and non-violator firms indicates that, on average, non-violator firms are less aggressive than violator firms, with these latter ones having cash outflows for tax payments lower than 7 percentage points than firms that do not incurr debt covenant violation.[7] The mean GAAP ETR*Vol* is 0.047

---

[6]The slight difference between the mean value provided by Guenther et al. (2017) and that one presented in this study may be attributed to differences in the sample size ($n = 25{,}669$ in Guenther et al. (2017) and in the time frame investigated (years = 1993–2016 in Guenther et al., 2017).

[7]There is also large variations in Cash Flow ETR values for the two sub-groups of firms across the life cycle stages. For introduction firms, the mean value Cash ETR value for non-violator firms is 0.064 (6.4%), while of 0.091 (9.1%) for violator firms. In the growth stage, non-violator firms have

Table 5.2 Descriptive statistics

	Non-violators					Violators						Sample total				
	Mean	Median	p25	p75	SD	Mean	Median	p25	p75	SD	Mean-in-Diff	Mean	Median	p25	p75	SD
Explanatory variables																
GAAP ETRVol$_{i,(t,t-4)}$	0.046	0.029	0.012	0.064	0.047	0.051	0.031	0.012	0.074	0.053	-0.00531*** (-10.10)	0.047	0.029	0.012	0.066	0.049
Cash Flow ETR$_{i,t}$	0.241	0.188	0.031	0.424	0.238	0.170	0.086	0.000	0.302	0.228	0.0711*** (27.79)	0.227	0.167	0.020	0.401	0.237
Control variables																
WC_TA$_{i,t}$	0.233	0.208	0.058	0.393	0.213	0.265	0.256	0.110	0.421	0.208	-0.0319*** (-13.84)	0.240	0.219	0.067	0.400	0.213
RE_TA$_{i,t}$	0.112	0.202	0.039	0.402	0.457	-0.044	0.102	-0.094	0.274	0.603	0.156*** (29.36)	0.080	0.181	0.018	0.377	0.494
Ebit_TA$_{i,t}$	0.081	0.089	0.049	0.140	0.081	0.051	0.068	0.020	0.113	0.101	0.0295*** (31.80)	0.075	0.085	0.043	0.135	0.086
MV_TL$_{i,t}$	3.363	1.685	0.837	4.359	3.674	3.070	1.667	0.714	3.892	3.444	0.293*** (7.43)	3.303	1.681	0.837	4.264	3.630
S_TA$_{i,t}$	1.035	0.933	0.575	1.431	0.572	1.257	1.206	0.809	1.752	0.562	-0.222*** (-35.95)	1.080	0.988	0.614	1.506	0.577

Asterisks reported in the Mean-in-Diff column represent the following *p*-values: * *p*-value <0.05; ** *p*-value <0.01; *** *p*-value <0.001

(4.7%). Specifically, the mean GAAP ETR*Vol* is equal to 0.046 (4.6%) for the subsample of non-violator firms and equal to 0.051 (5.1 %) for the subsample of violator firms. The values of the GAAP ETR volatility variable indicate that non-violator are less likely to engage risky tax avoidance practices that increase the volatility of the effective tax rates. This empirical evidence is complementary to that one obtained using the Cash Flow ETR, suggesting that non-violator firms are less likely to engage risky tax avoidance activities. Reported t-statistics show that the mean-in-difference of our tax avoidance proxies between violator and non-violator firms are highly statistically significant (p-value < 0.01). The descriptive statistics of the sample investigated suggest that, on average, violator firms show higher level of tax avoidance.

Descriptive statistics of the financial ratios included in the analysis as control variables show that, on average, firms violating debt covenant have, as expectable, a lower level of profitability (as highlighted by the ratio between retained earnings and total assets, and the ratio between EBIT and total assets), and a lower of market value on the total liabilities, while they have a higher level of net liquid assets and net sales on total assets.[8]

5.3.2 Univariate Analysis

Table 5.3 shows the Spearman correlation coefficients. The univariate analysis (displayed at Table 5.3) shows that our explanatory variables are highly statistically correlated with the dependent variable. Also, the dependent variable is highly correlated with all the various stages of corporate life cycle (with a significance level <0.01), except for the growth stage and the shake-out stage. Specifically, *Violation* is highly positively correlated with the introduction and the decline stage of the corporate life cycle, whereas it is highly negatively correlated mature phase.

---

a mean Cash Flow ETR value of 0.253 (25.3%) and of 0.246 (24.6%) for the violator subgroup. Mature firms show a mean Cash Flow ETR of 0.264, with an important and statistically significant difference between violators (18.9%) and non-violator firms (27.6%). Finally, firms in the decline stage that violate debt covenant have a Cash Flow ETR of 0.092 (9.2%) compared to the mean cash flow ETR of 0.105 (10.5%) for the violator firms. These descriptive statistics are consistent with prior findings that firms engage higher level of tax avoidance when in the introduction and decline stage of the corporate life cycle (Hasan et al., 2017).

[8] A higher level of the WC_TA and S_TA for violator firms may be surprising at first. However, as suggested by prior literature, not all the firms experiencing debt covenant violation are actually financially distressed firms (Roberts & Sufi, 2009). Hence, the descriptive statistics for a sample of violator and non-violator firms may diverge from that of financially distressed and non-financially distressed firms. Moreover, it should also be pointed out that the effect of sales on debt covenant violation and default is ambiguous and it can vary from model to model (Shumway, 2001). Using hazard models, Shumway (2001) finds a positive association between S_TA and bankruptcy, although not statistically significant in most of the models.

Table 5.3 Correlation results

Covariates	Violation	Introduction	Growth	Mature	Shakeout	Decline	GAAPETRVol$_{i,(t-4)}$	Cash Flow ETR$_{i,t}$	WC_TA$_{i,t}$	RE_TA$_{i,t}$	Ebit_TA$_{i,t}$	MV_TL$_{i,t}$	S_TA$_{i,t}$
Dependent variable													
Violation	1												
Moderator variables													
Introduction	0.119***	1											
Growth	-0.00477	-0.187***	1										
mature	-0.0752***	-0.255***	-0.668***	1									
Shakeout	-0.00442	-0.00234	-0.00612	-0.00833	1								
Decline	0.0442***	-0.0460***	-0.121***	-0.164***	-0.00150	1							
Explanatory variables													
GAAPETRVol$_{i,(t-4)}$	0.0441***	0.0281***	0.00241	-0.0518***	-0.00188	0.0375***	1						
Cash Flow ETR$_{i,t}$	-0.121***	-0.277***	0.0727***	0.139***	0.00243	-0.163***	-0.139***	1					
Control variables													
WC_TA$_{i,t}$	0.0604***	0.0630***	-0.0504***	-0.0787***	-0.00859*	0.0578***	0.0167***	0.0298***	1				
RE_TA$_{i,t}$	-0.127***	-0.105***	0.0272***	0.127***	-0.0204***	-0.152***	-0.144***	0.235***	0.0737***	1			
Ebit_TA$_{i,t}$	-0.138***	-0.224***	0.0546***	0.227***	0.00534	-0.297***	-0.118***	0.337***	0.0445***	0.357***	1		
MV_TL$_{i,t}$	-0.0325*	-0.0364***	0.0684***	-0.0734***	-0.00312	-0.000405	-0.0110*	0.0374***	0.526***	0.0522***	0.168***	1	
S_TA$_{i,t}$	0.155***	0.0619***	-0.141***	0.136***	-0.0118**	-0.0322***	-0.0989***	0.0968***	0.141***	0.00470	0.148***	-0.0789***	1

There is no significant correlation between bankruptcy and the growth and shake-out stage.

The explanatory variable GAAP ETRVol$_{i,(t,t-4)}$ is highly positively correlated with the introduction and the growth stage and decline stage, and negatively correlated with the mature stage and the decline stage. There is no correlation with the shake-out stage. *Cash Flow* ETR$_{i,t}$ shows a negative correlation with the introduction, growth, and decline stage (with a high degree of statistical significance), and a highly negative correlation with the mature stage. There is no correlation with the growth and shakeout stages.

All the control variables exhibit statistically significant association with bankruptcy in the expected direction with the dependent variable.

5.3.3 Results from the Main Analyses

Table 5.4 reports the main results obtained running the main analyses. Specifically, Table 5.4 Columns 1 and 2 report the results for the logit model, whereas Table 5.4 Columns 3 and 4 report the results for the hazard model. For brevity reason, Table 5.4 reports only the coefficients for tax avoidance; tax avoidance and life cycle; tax avoidance, life cycle and their interaction. In both the case, the financial ratios excerpted from the Altman model (Altman, 1968) conserve their statistical significance and expected direction in all the model developed (untabulated).

Table 5.4 Columns 1 and 3 reports the results obtained by running the model using a 1-year lagged GAAP ETR$Vol_{(t, t - 4)}$ as proxy for tax avoidance. Results show that tax avoidance is positively associated with debt covenant violation, with a high degree of statistical significance (p-value < 0.01). The results are in line with a risk-increasing view of tax avoidance and with previous research on tax avoidance and capital structure in different setting (Hasan et al., 2014; Dhawan et al., 2020).[9] These results suggest that higher level of tax avoidance is positively associated with the risk of violating debt covenant as the main effect in the sample. However, firms in the introduction and decline stage show a different behavior compared with the main effect. For these firms, higher level of tax avoidance is associated with a lower risk of covenant violation (p-value < 0.1 for the introduction stage and p-value < 0.05). Table 5.4 Columns 2 and 4 reports the results obtained by running the model and using a 1-year lagged Cash Flow ETR as a proxy for tax avoidance. Results show that tax avoidance (i.e., Cash Flow ETR) is positively (i.e., negatively) associated with debt covenant violation as the main effect in the sample. These

---

[9]Dhawan et al. (2020) examined the relationship between a battery of tax avoidance proxies and the risk of bankruptcy. Among the measures used to proxy for tax avoidance, these authors also investigate the GAAP ETR Volatility, showing that this variable (as all the other proxies investigated) is positively associated with the risk of bankruptcy. The study of Dhawan et al. (2020) was conducted on a sample of Australian public firms. The debt covenant violation likelihood and the bankruptcy risk are very related concepts (Habib et al., 2020).

Table 5.4 Main analysis: pooled regression

	Pred. sign	Debt covenant violation			
		(1)	(2)	(3)	(4)
Cash Flow ETR$_{i,\,t-1}$	(?)		−0.805***		−0.741***
			(0.176)		(0.155)
GAAP ETRVol$_{i,\,(t-1,\,t-5)}$	(?)	2.856***		2.440***	
		(0.925)		(0.759)	
Introduction × *Cash Flow ETR*$_{i,\,t-1}$	(+)		0.743***		0.684***
			(0.234)		(0.194)
Growth × *Cash Flow ETR*$_{i,\,t-1}$	(?)		−0.0164		−0.0106
			(0.199)		(0.173)
Mature × *Cash Flow ETR*$_{i,\,t-1}$	(−)		−0.537***		−0.502***
			(0.191)		(0.169)
Decline × *Cash Flow ETR*$_{i,\,t-1}$	(+)		1.085***		1.061***
			(0.302)		(0.250)
Introduction × *GAAP ETRVol*$_{i,\,(t-1,\,t-5)}$	(−)	−2.122*		−1.747*	
		(1.266)		(0.979)	
Growth × *GAAP ETRVol*$_{i,\,(t-1,\,t-5)}$	(?)	−1.025		−0.795	
		(1.011)		(0.836)	
Mature × *GAAP ETRVol*$_{i,\,(t-1,\,t-5)}$	(+)	0.502		0.614	
		(0.973)		(0.811)	
Decline × *GAAP ETRVol*$_{i,\,(t-1,\,t-5)}$	(−)	−3.903**		−2.912**	
		(1.532)		(1.238)	
Observations		47,565	49,294	47,565	49,294
Estimation model		Logit	Logit	Hazard	Hazard
Model controls		Yes	Yes	Yes	Yes
Life cycle dummies		Yes	Yes	Yes	Yes
Year fixed effects		Yes	Yes	Yes	Yes
Industry fixed effects		Yes	Yes	Yes	Yes
Standard errors clustered BY		Firm	Firm	Firm	Firm

This table reports the estimated coefficients obtained by using debt covenant violation as an alternative definition of the dependent variable. The table reports the results obtained by regressing the model with a dependent binary variable identifying debt covenant violation. Specifically, debt covenant violation is a dummy variable taking value of 1 for each firm-year observation of a firm violating a debt covenant, and 0 otherwise. Columns 1 and 3 report the results obtained by using a 1-year lagged G.A.A.P. effective tax rate volatility (GAAP ETRVol$_{i,\,(t,\,t-4)}$) as explanatory variable for tax avoidance. Column 2–4 report the results obtained by using the cash flow ETR as a measure for tax avoidance. Control variables used in the models are financial ratios taken from the standard Altman's model (Altman, 1968). All control variables included in the model are lagged at 1 year. All the columns reported in the table show the results obtained by running the model and including life cycle, tax avoidance, and the interaction of each stage of the corporate life cycle for tax avoidance. Column 1 and Column 2 show the results obtained by running the Altman logit model. Column 3 and Column 4 report the results obtained by estimating the Altman Hazard model. All the variables are winsorized at 1 and 99% to avoid the impact of outliers. Robust standard errors in parentheses. ***$p < 0.01$, **$p < 0.05$, *$p < 0.1$

results suggest that higher level of tax avoidance increases the risk of a debt covenant violation. However, firms in the introduction and decline stage show a different behavior compared with the main effect on the whole sample. For these firms, a higher level of tax avoidance is associated with a lower risk of violating debt covenant. These results are high statistically significant with a p-value < 0.01 for both the stages. The results also show that mature firms are penalized by higher level of tax avoidance. For firms in the mature stage, a higher level of tax avoidance magnifies the risk of covenant violation compared with the sample main effect (p-value < 0.01). These results provide empirical confirmation for the hypotheses. Collectively, the results indicate that firms in corporate life cycle stages characterized by low or absent agency conflicts, like the introductory and decline stage, could benefit from higher level of tax avoidance. Conversely, firms in corporate life cycle stages associated with high agency conflicts, are less likely to benefit from tax avoidance. Particularly, for firms in the mature stage, a higher risky tax avoidance is likely to magnify the risk of covenant violation, possibly due to higher risk of managerial discretion embedded in such activities.

5.3.4   Results from the Life Cycle-Wise Analyses

Following prior studies on corporate life cycle (e.g., Hasan et al., 2017), I also re-run the main model by developing single regressions for each stage of the corporate life cycle. Specifically, instead of including the life cycle dummy variables all together, I included each of them one by one. Then, I interacted each life cycle stage for the proxies of tax avoidance used. Table 5.5 (Panel A) shows the results for the Hazard model, while Table 5.5 (Panel B) shows the results obtained using the logit model. As for the main pooled results shown in Table 5.4, Table 5.5, Panel A and B, show only the coefficients of tax avoidance, tax avoidance and corporate life cycle and the interaction between the two variables. In both the case, the financial ratios included in the model conserve their statistical significance and expected direction (untabulated). Panel A and B (Columns 1) show the results obtained by running the main model and incorporating a proxy for tax avoidance (i.e., GAAP ETR Volatility), in addition to the corporate life cycle. The results show that the coefficient associated to the variable of tax avoidance (i.e., GAAP ETRVol) remains highly statistically significant and positively associated to debt covenant violation, when the corporate life cycle is also considered (p-value < 0.01). From Column 2–5, Table 5.5 (Panel A and B) reports the results obtained by adding the information on corporate life cycle and the interaction of each stage for the proxy of tax avoidance included. Column 2 report the results at the introduction stage; columns 3 reports the results for the growth stage; column 4 reports the results for the mature stage, while column 5 reports the results for the decline stage. Results indicate that the variable of tax avoidance is highly statistically significant and positively associated to financial default risk (p-value < 0.01). These results indicate that, on average, higher level of risky tax avoidance increases the likelihood of facing a debt covenant violation.

Table 5.5 Main life cycle-wise analyses using debt covenant violation

Panel A: hazard model	Debt covenant violation									
	GAAP ETR volatility					Cash Flow ETR				
	Tax model	Introduction	Growth	Mature	Decline	Tax model	Introduction	Growth	Mature	Decline
GAAP ETRVol$_{i, (t-1, t-5)}$	2.189***	2.311***	2.434***	1.521***	2.331***					
	(0.396)	(0.413)	(0.433)	(0.424)	(0.401)					
Cash Flow ETR$_{i, t-1}$						−0.879***	−0.950***	−0.945***	−0.586***	−0.930***
						(0.0778)	(0.0839)	(0.0858)	(0.0814)	(0.0799)
Introduction × GAAP ETRVol$_{i, (t-1, t-5)}$		−1.633**								
		(0.734)								
Introduction × Cash Flow ETR$_{i, t-1}$							0.902***			
							(0.143)			
Growth × GAAP ETRVol$_{i, (t-1, t-5)}$			−0.827							
			(0.518)							
Growth × Cash Flow ETR$_{i, t-1}$								0.211*		
								(0.114)		
Mature × GAAP ETR$_{i, (t-1, t-5)}$				1.538***						
				(0.509)						
Mature × Cash Flow ETR$_{i, t-1}$									−0.647***	
									(0.112)	
Decline × GAAP ETRVol$_{i, (t-1, t-5)}$					−2.785**					
					(1.168)					
Decline × Cash Flow ETR$_{i, t-1}$										1.289***
										(0.219)
Observations	47,565	47,565	47,565	47,565	47,565	49,294	49,294	49,294	49,294	49,294
Stage-specific life cycle dummies	Yes	Yes	Yes	Yes	Yes	Yes	Yes	Yes	Yes	Yes
Model controls	Yes	Yes	Yes	Yes	Yes	Yes	Yes	Yes	Yes	Yes
Year Fixed Effects	Yes	Yes	Yes	Yes	Yes	Yes	Yes	Yes	Yes	Yes
Industry fixed effects	Yes	Yes	Yes	Yes	Yes	Yes	Yes	Yes	Yes	Yes
Standard error clustered by	Firm	Firm	Firm	Firm	Firm	Firm	Firm	Firm	Firm	Firm

| Panel B: logit model | Debt covenant violation | | | | | | | | | |
| | GAAP ETR volatility | | | | | Cash Flow ETR | | | | |
	Tax Model	Introduction	Growth	Mature	Decline	Tax Model	Introduction	Growth	Mature	Decline
GAAP ETRVol$_{i,(t-1,t-5)}$	2.488***	2.570***	2.793***	1.744***	2.653***					
	(0.480)	(0.493)	(0.523)	(0.525)	(0.485)					
Cash Flow ETR$_{i,t-1}$						−0.976***	−1.037***	−1.052***	−0.668***	−1.027***
						(0.0875)	(0.0932)	(0.0959)	(0.0942)	(0.0898)
Introduction × GAAP ETRVol$_{i,(t-1,t-5)}$		−1.848*								
		(0.984)								
Introduction × Cash Flow ETR$_{i,t-1}$							0.986***			
							(0.179)			
Growth × GAAP ETRVol$_{i,(t-1,t-5)}$			−0.993							
			(0.620)							
Growth × Cash Flow ETR$_{i,t-1}$								0.248*		
								(0.131)		
Mature × GAAP ETR$_{i,(t-1,t-5)}$				1.636***						
				(0.601)						
Mature × Cash Flow ETR$_{i,t-1}$									−0.668***	
									(0.125)	
Decline × GAAP ETRVol$_{i,(t-1,t-5)}$					−3.748***					
					(1.448)					
Decline × Cash Flow ETR$_{i,t-1}$										1.337***
										(0.270)
Observations	47,565	47,565	47,565	47,565	47,565	49,294	49,294	49,294	49,294	49,294
Stage-specific life cycle dummies	Yes	Yes	Yes	Yes	Yes	Yes	Yes	Yes	Yes	Yes
Model controls	Yes	Yes	Yes	Yes	Yes	Yes	Yes	Yes	Yes	Yes
Year fixed effects	Yes	Yes	Yes	Yes	Yes	Yes	Yes	Yes	Yes	Yes
Industry fixed effects	Yes	Yes	Yes	Yes	Yes	Yes	Yes	Yes	Yes	Yes
Standard error clustered by	Firm	Firm	Firm	Firm	Firm	Firm	Firm	Firm	Firm	Firm

However, consistently with the results from the pooled regressions reported in Table 5.4, both Panel A (Hazard Model) and Panel B (Logit Model) of Table 5.5 show that the interaction of each stage of the corporate life cycle with the proxy for tax avoidance is moderated by the corporate life cycle. Specifically, the interactions terms between introduction stage and decline stage with the tax avoidance are highly statistically significant and negatively associated with financial default risk. The negative coefficient suggests that higher level of risky tax avoidance in the introduction and decline stage are associated with a lower likelihood of violating debt covenant. Table 5.5 Columns 6–10 (Panel A and B) shows complementary results.

Panel A and B (Columns 6) show the results obtained by running the main model and incorporating a proxy for tax avoidance (i.e., Cash Flow ETR), in addition to the corporate life cycle. The results show that the coefficient associated to the proxy used for tax avoidance (i.e., Cash Flow ETR) remains highly statistically significant and positively associated to debt covenant violation, when the corporate life cycle is also considered (p-value < 0.01). From Column 7–10, Table 5.5 (Panel A and B) reports the results obtained by adding the information on corporate life cycle and the interaction of each stage for the proxy of tax avoidance. Column 7 reports the results at the introduction stage; column 8 reports the results for the growth stage; column 9 reports the results for the mature stage, while column 10 reports the results for the decline stage. Results indicate that the variable of tax avoidance is highly statistically significant and positively associated to debt covenant violation (p-value < 0.01). These results indicate that, on average, higher level of tax avoidance increases the likelihood of facing a debt covenant violation. However, consistently with the results from the pooled regressions reported in Table 5.4, both Panel A (Hazard Model) and Panel B (Logit Model) of Table 5.5 show that the interaction of each stage of the corporate life cycle with the proxy for tax avoidance is moderated by the corporate life cycle. Specifically, the interactions terms between introduction stage and decline stage with Cash Flow ETR are highly statistically significant and negatively associated with debt covenant violation. The result indicates that a higher level of tax avoidance (i.e. lower effective tax rate) reduces the risk of debt covenant violation in the introduction and decline stage. By contrast, firms in the growth and mature stages do not show a different behavior compared with the main effect on the whole sample. Again, results from the life cycle-wise analyses furtherly confirm the hypothesis of the study. Collectively, the results of the analyses suggest that tax avoidance can be a powerful additional source of funding for firms in life cycle stages characterized by low or absent agency conflicts, like the introduction and decline stage; whilst it can engender a firm's risk in the stages of the corporate life cycle characterized by high agency conflicts.

5.4 Robustness and Endogeneity Checks

5.4.1 Different Operationalization of the Dependent Variable

I replicate the analyses using a different operational definition of debt covenant violation. In the main analyses, I define debt covenant violation as a dummy variable which takes value of 1 for each firm-year observations of a firm disclosing the violation of a debt covenant, and 0 otherwise. As a robustness check, I re-run the main analyses using a different operational definition of the debt covenant violation dependent variable. Specifically, I define debt covenant violation as a dummy variable which takes value of 1 for the firm-year observation in which the firm violates a debt covenant, and 0 otherwise. Overall, the results from the robustness test confirm previous findings obtained from the main analysis (see Table 5.6). I also obtained broadly consistent results when using GAAP ETR*Vol* as explanatory variable (untabulated).

5.4.2 Propensity Score Matching Analysis

It can be argued that a higher level of leverage might incentivize firms to use tax avoidance in order to reduce the debt covenant violation likelihood. At the same time, the average tax rate is endogenous to the firm (Graham et al., 1998; Richardson et al., 2015). Thus, a potential reverse causality could arise from firms' leverage and tax avoidance. In this study, besides using lagged values of the explanatory variable, I also addressed potential endogeneity issues by means of a propensity score matching (PSM) analysis (Rosenbaum & Rubin, 1985; Angrist & Pischke, 2010; Shipman et al., 2017). Specifically, I re-run the main analyses using a matched sample including firms incurred into a debt covenant violation and a control sample of non-violator firm, with similar characteristics in terms of control variables used in the main model. Specifically, the propensity score matching analysis uses the working capital on total assets (WC_TA), the retained earnings on total assets (RE_TA); the earnings before interests and taxes on total assets (EBIT_TA); the market value of equity on total liabilities (MV_TL) and sales on total assets (S_TA) to build a matched sample of firms. I matched without replacement imposing a caliper distance of 0.01. The propensity score matching (PSM) analysis can mitigate potential issue of a sample selection bias (Shipman et al., 2017). In addition, it can also provide further assurance that the main results are still valid and robust also when comparing firms with similar level of size, performance, liquidity, leverage, industry, and year.

Table 5.7 shows the results obtained by running the logit model on a sub-sample of firms obtained with a propensity score matching approach and using the pooled approach. Results of the analyses confirm the main findings. Specifically, the propensity score matching (PSM) analysis shows that tax avoidance is positively

Table 5.6 Robustness check: analysis using a different definition of debt covenant violation

	Tax model	Debt covenant violation				
		Introduction	Growth	Mature	Decline	Pooled model
Cash Flow ETR$_{i,t-1}$	-1.549***	-1.667***	-1.662***	-1.164***	-1.669***	-1.578***
	(0.146)	(0.155)	(0.168)	(0.179)	(0.151)	(0.377)
Introduction × Cash Flow ETR$_{i,t-1}$		1.182***				0.979**
		(0.350)				(0.489)
Growth × Cash Flow ETR$_{i,t-1}$			0.460			0.290
			(0.303)			(0.457)
Mature × Cash Flow ETR$_{i,t-1}$				-0.805***		-0.481
				(0.275)		(0.434)
Decline × Cash Flow ETR$_{i,t-1}$					1.964***	1.761***
					(0.430)	(0.553)
Observations	46,403	46,403	46,403	46,403	46,403	46,403
Model controls	Yes	Yes	Yes	Yes	Yes	Yes
Life cycle dummies	Yes	Yes	Yes	Yes	Yes	Yes
Year fixed effects	Yes	Yes	Yes	Yes	Yes	Yes
Industry fixed effects	Yes	Yes	Yes	Yes	Yes	Yes
Std errors cld. by	Firm	Firm	Firm	Firm	Firm	Firm

This table reports the life cycle-wise and pooled estimated coefficients obtained by running both the logit model and using an alternative definition of the dependent variable debt covenant violation variable. Specifically, the debt covenant violation dummy variable takes value of one for the firm-year observation in which the firm violates a debt covenant, and zero otherwise. Columns 1 ("Tax Model") report the results obtained by using a proxy for tax avoidance, without including the corporate life cycle. Columns 2–5 show the results of the life cycle-wise analysis, while Column 6 reports the results for the pooled model. All the variables are winsorized at 1 and 99% to avoid the impact of outliers. Robust standard errors in parentheses. *** $p < 0.01$, ** $p < 0.05$, * $p < 0.1$

Table 5.7 Propensity score matching approach

	Debt covenant violation	
	(1)	(2)
GAAP ETR$Vol_{(i, t-1, t-5)}$		3.301***
		(1.153)
Cash Flow ETR$_{i, t-1}$	−0.678***	
	(0.202)	
Introduction		
Introduction × GAAP ETR$Vol_{(i, t-1, t-5)}$		−3.766**
		(1.643)
Introduction × Cash Flow ETR$_{i, t-1}$	0.575**	
	(0.267)	
Growth		
Growth × GAAP ETR$Vol_{(i, t-1, t-5)}$		−1.694
		(1.311)
Growth × Cash Flow ETR$_{i, t-1}$	−0.0335	
	(0.229)	
Mature		
Mature × GAAP ETR$Vol_{(i, t-1, t-5)}$		0.491
		(1.249)
Mature × Cash Flow ETR$_{i, t-1}$	−0.567**	
	(0.221)	
Decline		
Decline × GAAP ETR$Vol_{(i, t-1, t-5)}$		−6.141***
		(2.319)
Decline × Cash Flow ETR$_{i, t-1}$	1.015***	
	(0.360)	
Observations	20,290	14,735
Control variables	Yes	Yes
Life cycle dummies	Yes	Yes
Year fixed effects	Yes	Yes
Industry fixed effects	Yes	Yes
Standard errors clustered by	Firm	Firm

This table reports the estimated coefficients obtained by running the pooled analysis on a matched sample retrieved through a propensity score matching analysis and using the logit model as estimation procedure. Column 1 shows the results obtained by using cash flow ETR as an explanatory variable, while and Column 2 show the results obtained by GAAP ETR Volatility as explanatory variable. All the variables are winsorized at 1% and 99% to avoid the impact of outliers. Robust standard errors in parentheses. $^{***}p < 0.01$, $^{**}p < 0.05$, $^{*}p < 0.1$

associated with debt covenant violation, as the main effect in the matched sample. However, the introduction and decline stage firms display a different behaviour compared to the matched sample. Firms in the introduction and decline stages engaging higher level of tax avoidance and/or taking more risky tax positions are likely to benefit of a lower likelihood of debt covenant violation. Conversely, higher levels of tax avoidance is not likely to be beneficial for firms in the growth and mature stage.[10]

Table 5.8 displays the results obtained by running the logit model on a sub-sample of firms obtained with a propensity score matching approach and using the life cycle-wise approach. The findings show that the there is a positive association between tax risk and debt covenant violation. Again, as for the main results, this finding suggests that higher level of tax risk, as featured by the volatility of effective tax rates, increases the likelihood of violating a debt covenant. However, this effect is moderated by the corporate life cycle. Specifically, the results of the moderation analysis show that the positive effect of tax risk on the debt covenant violation likelihood is reversed for firms that are in the introduction and decline stage. For these firms, a higher level of tax risk (i.e., GAAP ETR volatility) is likely to result in a lower likelihood of violating a debt covenant compared to the average effect in the sample. These results suggest that riskier tax positions (e.g., taking more aggressive tax positions with a higher likelihood of being challenged upon audit by the tax authority) may be beneficial to avoid debt covenant for firms in the introductory and decline. Alternatively, the result could suggest that lenders do not negatively perceive the volatility of effective tax rates when evaluating tax positions of firms in the introduction and decline stage. The results reported at Table 5.8 also show that firms in the growth stage show a different behavior compared to the main effect. Again, for these firms a higher level of tax risk is likely to reduce the probability of violating a debt covenant. It must be noted, however, that the coefficient on the growth stage is smaller compared to those of firms in introductory and decline stage, suggesting that the benefits of tax risk are likely to dissipate as firms enter the growth stage. Moreover, it has also to be noted that the coefficient on the growth stage is smaller compared to that one associated to the average effect in the sample (-1.356 vs. 2.945) and has lower statistical significance (p-value > 0.1 vs. p-value > 0.01). This result suggests that, although tax risk is negatively associated with the default likelihood in the growth stage show, firms in the growth stage are unlikely to completely offset the main risk-increasing effect. Compared with the abovementioned life cycle stages, the analysis shows that mature firms do not exhibit any differential behavior with respect to main effect. For these firms, higher level of tax risk is likely to magnify the probability of violating a debt covenant. Collectively, the results of the analyses furtherly confirm main findings and provide empirical support for the paper's hypotheses. I replicate the PSM-based life cycle-wise analysis also using the Cash Flow ETR as a proxy for tax avoidance.

---

[10] As a robustness test, I also replicate the PSM analysis related to GAAP ETR*Vol* (see model 2) by matching also for the level of GAAP ETR, in addition to working capital on total assets, retained earnings on total assets; earnings before interests and taxes on total assets; market value of equity on total liabilities, and sales on total assets. The results obtained provide results consistent with those shown in column 2, Table 5.4 (untabulated). These results indicate that the debt covenant violation likelihood may also vary for firms that, although showing similar level of tax avoidance, may have different level of tax risk. At the same levels of tax avoidance, lenders may perceive firms with more volatile effective tax rates as riskier compared to those firms with less volatile effective tax rates.

Table 5.8 Addressing endogeneity: propensity score matching analysis

Panel A: Life-cycle-wise analysis using GAAP ETR volatility		Debt covenant violation			
	Pred. sign	Introduction	Growth	Mature	Decline
GAAP ETRVol$_{(i, t-1, t-5)}$	(+)	2.705***	2.945***	1.436**	2.676***
		(0.556)	(0.603)	(0.605)	(0.546)
Introduction × GAAP ETRVol$_{(i, t-1, t-5)}$	(−)	−3.193**			
		(1.273)			
Growth × GAAP ETRVol$_{(i, t-1, t-5)}$	(?)		1.356*		
			(0.815)		
Mature × GAAP ETRVol$_{(i, t-1, t-5)}$	(+)			2.391***	
				(0.776)	
Decline × GAAP ETRVol$_{(i, t-1, t-5)}$	(−)				5.468***
					(2.111)
Observations		14,735	14,735	14,735	14,735
Life cycle dummies		Yes	Yes	Yes	Yes
Model controls		Yes	Yes	Yes	Yes
Year fixed effects		Yes	Yes	Yes	Yes
Industry fixed effects		Yes	Yes	Yes	Yes
Standard error clustered by		Firm	Firm	Firm	Firm
Panel B: Life-cycle-wise analysis using Cash Flow ETR		Debt covenant violation			
	Pred. Sign	Introduction	Growth	Mature	Decline
Cash Flow ETR$_{i, t-1}$	(−)	−0.925***	−0.925***	−0.562***	−0.924***
		(0.0975)	(0.0975)	(0.101)	(0.0933)
Introduction × Cash Flow ETR$_{i, t-1}$	(+)	0.829***			
		(0.200)			
Growth × Cash Flow ETR$_{i, t-1}$	(?)		0.245*		
			(0.146)		
Mature × Cash Flow ETR$_{i, t-1}$	(−)			−0.680***	
				(0.140)	
Decline × Cash Flow ETR$_{i, t-1}$	(+)				1.286***
					(0.314)
Observations		20,290	20,290	20,290	20,290
Life cycle dummies		Yes	Yes	Yes	Yes
Model controls		Yes	Yes	Yes	Yes
Year fixed effects		Yes	Yes	Yes	Yes
Industry fixed effects		Yes	Yes	Yes	Yes
Standard error clustered by		Firm	Firm	Firm	Firm

This table reports the estimated coefficients obtained by running the life cycle-wise analysis on a matched sample of firms retrieved through a propensity score matching procedure and using the logit model as estimation procedure. Column 1 shows the results obtained by using cash flow ETR as an explanatory variable, while and Column 2 show the results obtained by GAAP ETR Volatility as explanatory variable. All the variables are winsorized at 1% and 99% to avoid the impact of outliers. Robust standard errors in parentheses. ***$p < 0.01$, **$p < 0.05$, *$p < 0.1$

In line with the results obtained with tax risk and with the main findings, Across the columns of Table 5.8, Panel B, it is shown that tax avoidance (i.e., Cash Flow ETR) has a positive (i.e., negative) association with debt covenant violation, as main effect for the whole sample. Again, however, this effect is reversed for firms in the introduction, growth, and decline stage. Particularly, the magnitude of the coefficients associated to these stages is consistent with those obtained through the PSM-based pooled analyses. This result furtherly indicates that the reverting effect of tax avoidance is highest for firms that are in the decline stage of the corporate life cycle, whilst it is only limited for firms that are in the growth stage. Mature firms do not show any reverting behavior compared with the main effect. By contrast, for these firms a higher level of tax avoidance can engender the risk of debt covenant violation. This result can also suggest that mature firms contribute to most of the risk-increasing effect observed in the sample.

5.5   Discussion and Conclusions

In this study, I have provided comprehensive empirical evidence on the association between tax avoidance and debt covenant violation, once considered the corporate life cycle. Basing on the Agency Theory (Jensen & Meckling, 1976; Jensen, 1986), the research argues that agency conflicts between shareholders and mangers change as the firms proceed along the stages of the corporate life cycle. In context with low agency conflicts between shareholders and managers, such as the introduction and decline stage, tax avoidance is likely to be used by managers as an activity beneficial to the firm's shareholders, useful to provide the firm with additional precautionary cash resources, thus reducing the risk of debt covenant violation. Conversely, in context of high agency conflicts between shareholders and managers, such as in the mature stage, tax avoidance is likely to be an activity complementary to rent extraction and diversion, managerial entrenchment, and wealth dissipation, thus increasing the risk of violating debt covenant.

The research has examined the association between tax avoidance and debt covenant violation as conditioned by the corporate life cycle, defined by means of cash flow patterns (Dickinson, 2011). After controlling for a set of financial ratios that prior literature has found to be associated with corporate default (Altman, 1968), the results of the analyses show that the association between tax avoidance and debt covenant violation varies depending on the stages of the corporate life cycle. Specifically, findings show that tax avoidance is positively associated with debt covenant violation in the mature stage. On the other hand, tax avoidance is negatively associated with risk of violation in the introduction and decline stage. The results hold to a battery of robustness and endogeneity checks.

To the extent that the level of free cash flow, as reflected by a firm's cash flow patterns, can be used as a proxy of the level of agency conflicts (Jensen, 1986; Owen & Yawson, 2010), the results of our analyses suggest that there is a positive association between tax avoidance and debt covenant violation in the stages of the corporate life cycle where there are greater agency conflicts between shareholders and managers. Conversely, there is a negative association between tax avoidance and debt covenant violation in the stages of the corporate life cycle where there are lower agency conflicts between shareholders and managers. Taken together, the results suggest that the association between tax avoidance and debt covenant violation is conditional to the stage of the corporate life cycle and to the level of agency conflicts associated to it. Overall, the findings are consistent with a life cycle-based interpretation of the Agency Theory (Jensen, 1986; DeAngelo et al., 2006; Filatotchev et al., 2006; O'Connor & Byrne, 2015).

This research can provide several important contributions to the academic literature. *First*, this study contributes to the still scant literature examining the association between tax avoidance, debt covenant and the related risk of default (Kim et al., 2010; Hasan et al., 2014; Platikanova, 2017). Compared to prior research, this study shows that the association between tax avoidance and debt covenant violation is not static. Although this study resumes an investigational line already pursued by Kim et al. (2010), this research differs from the paper of Kim et al. (2010) in several important ways. First, this study examines the question of whether tax avoidance is associated with debt covenant violation, according to the firm's life cycle stage. Kim et al. (2010) do not consider that different agency settings, as framed by a firm's life cycle stages, could change the way tax avoidance is associated to debt covenant violation. Moreover, this study uses a novel measure of cash tax avoidance which is considerably less afflicted by earnings management consideration compared to accrual-based effective tax rates used by Kim et al. (2010). Given that manipulation of the accruals is a frequent occurrence in firms approaching default, it is important to detach tax avoidance from earnings management. Hence, a cash flow-based definition of the effective tax rates, as the one used in this research, may have reasonably superior ability in identifying corporate tax avoidance that is not related to earnings management considerations (Guenther et al., 2017). To the extent the level of free cash flow, as reflected by the firm's cash flow patterns, signal agency conflicts (Jensen, 1986; Dickinson, 2011; Owen & Yawson, 2010), the results of the research suggest that the association between tax avoidance and debt covenant violation varies accordingly with the level of agency conflicts linked to each stage of the corporate life cycle.

Second, this study can contribute to the literature on managerial actions to address the risk of default across the various stages of the corporate life cycle. Prior life cycle studies show that managers may revert the risk of facing default that is contingent to the corporta life cycle stage by adopting corrective actions, such as CEO turnover, cash dividends reduction and layoff (Koh et al., 2015; Al-Hadi et al., 2019). Focusing on the debt covenant violation a type of default event (a.k.a., technical default) potentially affecting a firm during its life cycle stages, this study adds to this literature by showing that the likelihood of experiencing a default event, in the form of debt covenant violation, can be reverted in specific stages of the firm's life cycle of firms engaging higher tax avoidance (Habib et al., 2020). Future research may investigate whether this reverting effect also occurs for default events other than debt covenant violation including, for example, credit ratings downgrades, bankruptcy or liquidation. Additionally, future studies may assess usefulness of tax avoidance proxies in the financial distress forecasting (Ciampi et al., 2021)

Third, the results of this research can also add to the prior tax literature examining the consequences of tax avoidance for a firm's financial health (e.g., Graham & Tucker, 2006; Lin et al., 2014; Shevlin et al., 2020; Dhawan et al., 2020). Previous research investigates the effect of tax avoidance on a firm's financial health by using different proxies, including a firm's leverage ratios (Graham & Tucker, 2006; Lin et al., 2014); the cost of debt (Hasan et al., 2014; Shevlin et al., 2020); the cost of equity capital (Goh et al., 2016), and the risk of bankruptcy (Dhawan et al., 2020). These studies have provided competing views on the effect of tax avoidance for a firm's financial health, predicting either a positive or a negative effect. This study suggests that that the effect of tax avoidance for a firm's financial health can be positive in some life cycle stages (growth and mature) and negative in others (introduction and decline).

Finally, this research can also complement prior research investigating tax avoidance across the corporate life cycle (e.g., Drake, 2015; Hasan et al., 2017; Stam & Verbeeten, 2017). This stream of literature suggests that the corporate life cycle can affect a firm's tax avoidance propensity. In this study, I show that the stage of the corporate life cycle can also affects the outcomes of tax avoidance, at least with respect to a firm's debt covenant violation likelihood. Given the strong statistically significant association that exists between tax avoidance (and tax risk) and debt covenant violation, future studies may examine whether tax-based information retrievable from a firm's financial statements increase prediction ability of traditional financial distress models (e.g., Altman, 1968; Campbell et al., 2008; Ciampi et al., 2021), either when used alone as well as when interacted with the corporate life cycle stages (e.g., Lussier, 1995; Kane et al., 2003).

Besides contributing to the academic literature, the results of this research can also be informative for investors, analysts, lenders, and other market participants. This research suggests that corporate tax avoidance can be both involved in process of wealth creation (e.g., generation of additional cash resources) and in those in those of wealth dissipation (e.g., managerial rent extraction), depending on the level of agency conflicts between managers and shareholders associated to each stage of the corporate life cycle. In this way, this study suggests that corporate life cycle is an important feature to consider by corporate outsiders when examining firms' tax avoidance.

As any study, even this empirical research is not free from limitations.

A first important limitation related to this empirical investigation pertains to the assumption that that the separation between ownership and control and the related agency conflicts between the shareholders and the managers is (indirectly) captured by the corporate life cycle stages and their related cash flow patterns (i.e., the level of free cash flow available) (Jensen, 1986; Dickinson, 2011). This assumption is supported by prior literature examining the dynamic of agency conflicts and corporate governance structures as a function of the firm's evolution across the life cycle stages (Vos & Forlong, 1996; Filatotchev et al., 2006, Owen & Yawson, 2010; O'Connor & Byrne, 2015). However, it is still possible that, for firms in the same life cycle, a different corporate governance quality may moderate the observed results.[11] For example, while mature firms do not seem to benefit from tax avoidance to reduce the debt covenant violation likelihood, mature firms with sophisticated governance structure may display a different behavior. Future studies may delve in deep this analysis by examining whether corporate governance differences affect the tax avoidance-debt covenant violation for firms within the same corporate life cycle stage.

A second limitation of this research pertains to the sample time frame and to the empirical context investigated (i.e., US public firms). While it plausibly that the results presented may also hold by investigating different time frame of the same sample[12] and for different types of firms in different countries, it is not possible to rule out the possibility that a different country setting, or a different time frame, may confute these results. In this sense, future research may consider investigating the tax avoidance-debt covenant violation relationship with respect to different country settings and different types of firms.

References

Agarwal, R., & Audretsch, D. B. (2001). Does entry size matter? The impact of the life cycle and technology on firm survival. *The Journal of Industrial Economics, 49*(1), 21–43.

Al-Hadi, A., et al. (2019). Corporate social responsibility performance, financial distress and firm life cycle: Evidence from Australia. *Accounting and Finance, 59*(2), 961–989.

Altman, E. I. (1968). Financial ratios, discriminant analysis and the prediction of corporate bankruptcy. *The Journal of Finance, 23*, 589–609.

Altman, E. I., Hotchkiss, E., & Wang, W. (2019). *Corporate financial distress, restructuring, and bankruptcy: Analyze leveraged finance, distressed debt, and bankruptcy* (4th ed.). Wiley.

Angrist, J. D., & Pischke, J. (2010). The credibility revolution in empirical economics: How better research design is taking the con out of econometrics. *Journal of Economic Perspectives, 24*(2), 3–30.

Anthony, J. H., & Ramesh, K. (1992). Association between accounting performance measures and stock prices: A test of the life cycle hypothesis. *Journal of Accounting and Economics, 15*(2 and 3), 203–227.

Bayar, O., Huseynov, F., & Sardarli, S. (2018). Corporate governance, tax avoidance, and financial constraints. *Financial Management, 47*(3), 651–677.

Beaver, W. H., Cascino, S., Correia, M., & McNichols, M. F. (2018). Group affiliation and default prediction. *Management Science.* ISSN 0025-1909. https://doi.org/10.1287/mnsc.2018.3128

Beaver, W. H., Correia, M., & McNichols, M. F. (2010). Financial statement analysis and the prediction of financial distress. *Foundations and Trends in Accounting, 5*, 99–173.

---

[11] This research partially mitigates such concern by clustering standard errors at a firm level and matching analyses. However, a more grain-fined exploration of the impact of corporate governance differences at a firm level per each stage of the corporate life cycle is encouraged in order to confirm or on the contrary confute the results of this research.

[12] Using year-fixed effects regressions, I mitigate the issue that the results obtained would be contingent to the time frame investigated and to contingent macroeconomic or political external variables.

Bellovary, J., Giacomino, D., & Akers, M. (2007). A review of bankruptcy prediction studies: 1930 to present. *Journal of Financial Education, 33*, 1–42.

Beneish, M. D., & Press, E. (1995). The resolution of technical default. *The Accounting Review, 70*, 337–353.

Black, E. (2003). Usefulness of financial statement components in valuation: an examination of start-up and growth firms. *Venture Capital: An International Journal of Entrepreneurial Finance, 5*(1), 47–69.

Blaylock, B. S. (2016). Is tax avoidance associated with economically significant rent extraction among US firms? *Contemporary Accounting Research, 33*(3), 1013–1043.

Blouin, J. (2014). Defining and measuring tax planning aggressiveness. *National Tax Journal, 67* (4), 875–899.

Campbell, J. Y., Hilscher, J., & Szilagyi, J. (2008). In search of distress risk. *The Journal of Finance, 63*, 2899–2939. https://doi.org/10.1111/j.1540-6261.2008.01416.x

Chava, S., & Jarrow, R. (2004). Bankruptcy Prediction with Industry Effects. *Review of Finance, 8*, 537–569. https://doi.org/10.1093/rof/8.4.537

Chod, J. (2017). Inventory, risk shifting, and trade credit. *Management Science, 63*(10), 3207–3225.

Ciampi, F., Giannozzi, A., Marzi, G., & Altman, E. I. (2021). Rethinking SME default prediction: a systematic literature review and future perspectives. *Scientometrics, 126*, 2141–2188.

Christensen, D. M., Kenchington, D. G., & Laux, R. C. (2022). How do most low ETR firms avoid paying taxes? *Review of Accounting Studies, 27*(2), 570–606.

DeAngelo, H., DeAngelo, L., & Stulz, R. M. (2006). Dividend policy and the earned/contributed capital mix: A test of the life-cycle theory. *Journal of Financial Economics, 81*(2), 227–254.

Demerjian, P. R., & Owens, E. L. (2016). Measuring the probability of financial covenant violation in private debt contracts. *Journal of Accounting and Economics, 61*(2-3), 433–447.

Dhawan, A., Kim, M. H., & Ma, L. (2020). Effect of corporate tax avoidance activities on firm bankruptcy risk. *Journal of Contemporary Accounting and Economics, 16*(2), 100187.

Dickinson, V. (2011). Cash flow patterns as a proxy for firm life cycle. *The Accounting Review, 86*(6), 1969–1994.

Drake, K. (2015). *Does firm life cycle explain the relation between book-tax differences and earnings persistence?* Working Paper. Retrieved from https://oatd.org/oatd/record?record=oai %5C%3Aarizonastate%5C%3A15021

Drake, K. D., Lusch, S. J., & Stekelberg, J. (2019). Does tax risk affect investor valuation of tax avoidance? *Journal of Accounting, Auditing and Finance, 34*(1), 151176.

Drake, K. D., & Martin, M. (2018). *Implementing relative performance evaluation: The role of life cycle peers.* Working paper. Available at SSRN https://ssrn.com/abstract=2822388.

Dyreng, S. D., Hillegeist, S. A., & Penalva, F. (2022). Earnings management to avoid debt covenant violations and future performance. *European Accounting Review, 31*(2), 311–343.

Faff, R., Kwok, W. C., Podolski, E. J., & Wong, G. (2016). Do corporate policies follow a life-cycle? *Journal of Banking and Finance, 69*, 95–107.

Filatotchev, I., Toms, S., & Wright, M. (2006). The firm's strategic dynamics and corporate governance lifecycle. *International Journal of Managerial Finance, 2*, 256–279.

Franz, D. R., HassabElnaby, H. R., & Lobo, G. J. (2014). Impact of proximity to debt covenant violation on earnings management. *Review of Accounting Studies, 19*, 473–505.

Gam, Y. K., & Liu, C. (2022). *Bank relationship and contractual flexibility: Evidence from covenant enforcement.* Available at SSRN 3486614.

Goh, B. W., Lee, J., Lim, C. Y., & Shevlin, T. (2016). The effect of corporate tax avoidance on the cost of equity. *The Accounting Review, 91*(6), 1647–1670.

Gort, M., & Klepper, S. (1982). Time paths in the diffusion of product innovations. *Economic Journal, 92*(367), 630–653.

Graham, J. R., Lemmon, M. L., & Schallheim, J. S. (1998). Debt, leases, taxes, and the endogeneity of corporate tax status. *The Journal of Finance, 53*(1), 131–162. https://doi.org/10.1111/ 0022-1082.55404

Graham, J., & Tucker, A. (2006). Tax shelters and corporate debt policy. *Journal of Financial Economics, 81*, 563–594.

Guenther, D. A., Matsunaga, S. R., & Williams, B. M. (2017). Is tax avoidance related to firm risk? *The Accounting Review, 92*(1), 115–136.

Habib, A., Costa, M. D., Huang, H. J., Bhuiyan, M. B. U., & Sun, L. (2020). Determinants and consequences of financial distress: review of the empirical literature. *Accounting and Finance, 60*, 1023–1075.

Habib, A., & Hasan, M. M. (2019). Corporate life cycle research in accounting, finance and corporate governance: A survey, and directions for future research. *International Review of Financial Analysis, 61(C)*, 188–201.

Hanlon, M., & Heitzman, S. (2010). A review of tax research. *Journal of Accounting and Economics, 50*(2 and 3), 127–178.

Hasan, M. M., Al-Hadi, A., Taylor, G., & Richardson, G. (2017). Does a firm's life cycle explain its propensity to engage in corporate tax avoidance? *European Accounting Review, 26*(3), 469–501. https://doi.org/10.1080/09638180.2016.1194220

Hasan, I., Hoi, C.-K. S., Wu, Q., & Zhang, H. (2014). Beauty is in the eye of the beholder: The effect of corporate tax avoidance on the cost of bank loans. *Journal of Financial Economics, 113*(1), 109–130.

Heitzman, S. M., & Ogneva, M. (2019). Industry tax planning and stock returns. *The Accounting Review, 94*(5), 219–246. https://doi.org/10.2308/accr-52361

Jaggi, B., & Lee, P. (2002). Earnings management response to debt covenant violations and debt restructuring. *Journal of Accounting, Auditing and Finance, 17*(4), 295–324.

Jensen, M. C. (1986). Agency costs of free cash flow, corporate finance, and takeovers. *The American Economic Review, 76*, 323–329.

Jensen, M. C., & Meckling, W. H. (1976). Theory of the firm: Managerial behavior, agency costs and ownership structure. *Journal of Financial Economics, 3*(4), 305–360.

Kane, G. D., Richardson, F. M., & Velury, U. (2003). The role of corporate life cycle in the prediction of corporate financial distress. *Commercial Lending Review, 18*, 26.

Kim, J.-B., Li, O. Z., & Li, Y. (2010). *Corporate tax avoidance and bank loan contracting*. Working paper, City University of Hong Kong, National University of Singapore, and Arizona State University.

Koh, S., Durand, R. B., Dai, L., & Chang, M. (2015). Financial distress: Lifecycle and corporate restructuring. *Journal of Corporate Finance, 33*, 19–33.

Lin, S., Tong, N., & Tucker, A. L. (2014). Corporate tax aggression and debt. *Journal of Banking and Finance, 40*, 227–241.

Lussier, R. N. (1995). A nonfinancial business success versus failure prediction model for young firms. *Journal of Small Business Management, 33*(1), 8–20.

Miller, D., & Friesen, P. (1984). A longitudinal study of the corporate life cycle. *Management Science, 30*(10), 1161–1183.

Molina, C. A., & Preve, L. A. (2009). Trade receivables policy of distressed firms and its effect on the costs of financial distress. *Financial Management, 38*(3), 663–686.

Molina, C. A., & Preve, L. A. (2012). An empirical analysis of the effect of financial distress on trade credit. *Financial Management, 41*(1), 187–205.

Moore, J. A., & Xu, L. (2018). Book-tax differences and costs of private debt. *Advances in Accounting, 42*, 70–82.

Muñoz-Izquierdo, N., Laitinen, E. K., Camacho-Miñano, M. D. M., & Pascual-Ezama, D. (2020). Does audit report information improve financial distress prediction over Altman's traditional Z-Score model? *Journal of International Financial Management and Accounting, 31*(1), 65–97.

O'Connor, T., & Byrne, J. (2015). Governance and the corporate life-cycle. *International Journal of Managerial Finance, 11*(1), 23–43. https://doi.org/10.1108/IJMF-03-2013-0033

Owen, S., & Yawson, A. (2010). Corporate life cycle and M&A activity. *Journal of Banking and Finance, 34*(2), 427–440.

Platikanova, P. (2017). Debt maturity and tax avoidance. *European Accounting Review, 26*(1), 97–124.

Quinn, S. L. (2019). *American bonds*. Princeton University Press.

Richardson, G., Grantley, T., & Roman, L. (2015). The impact of financial distress on corporate tax avoidance spanning the global financial crisis: Evidence from Australia. *Economic Modelling, 44(C)*, 44–53.

Roberts, M. R., & Sufi, A. (2009). Renegotiation of financial contracts: Evidence from private credit agreements. *Journal of Financial Economics, 93*(2), 159–184.

Rosenbaum, P. R., & Rubin, D. B. (1985). Constructing a control group using multivariate matched sampling methods that incorporate the propensity score. *The American Statistician, 39*(1), 33–38.

Shevlin, T., Urcan, O., & Vasvari, F. P. (2020). Corporate tax avoidance and debt costs. *Journal of the American Taxation Association, 42*(2), 117–143.

Shipman, J. E., Swanquist, Q. T., & Whited, R. L. (2017). Propensity score matching in accounting research. *The Accounting Review, 92*(1), 213–244.

Shumway, T. (2001). Forecasting bankruptcy more accurately: A simple hazard model. *Journal of Business, 74*(1), 101–124.

Stam, E., & Verbeeten, F. (2017). Tax compliance over the firm life course. *International Small Business Journal, 35*(1), 99–115.

Taylor, P. (2013). What do we know about the role of financial reporting in debt contracting and debt covenants? *Accounting and Business Research, 43*(4), 386–417.

Vergara, R. (2010). Taxation and private investment: Evidence for Chile. *Applied Economics, 42*(6), 717–725.

Vos, E., & Forlong, C. (1996). The agency advantage of debt over the lifecycle of the firm. *The Journal of Entrepreneurial Finance, 5*(3), 193–211.

Wang, F., Xu, S., Sun, J., & Cullinan, C. P. (2020). Corporate Tax avoidance: A literature review and Research Agenda. *Journal of Economic Surveys., 34*(4), 793–811.

Wooldridge, J. M. (2002). *Econometric analysis of cross section and panel data*. MIT Press.

Zhang, Z. (2019). Bank interventions and trade credit: evidence from debt covenant violations. *Journal of Financial and Quantitative Analysis, 54*(5), 2179–2207.

Zimmerman, J. L. (1983). Taxes and firm size. *Journal of Accounting and Economics, 5*, 119–149.

Chapter 6
Final Remarks

Keywords Tax avoidance · Capital structure · Financing decisions · Agency conflicts

6.1 Summary

This monograph examines the academic literature on the implications of tax avoidance activities for the corporate capital structure, providing novel evidence on the effect that such activities have on the debt covenant violation likelihood at each stage of the firm's life cycle.

Financial covenants are one of the common contingencies of debt agreements for many firms, requiring them and their managers to attain to specific accounting-based metrics set by the lenders (Demerjian & Owens, 2016). Prior literature suggests that apposition of debt covenants helps the borrower to get easier access to debt financing and to increase its creditability towards the lender, alleviating agency conflicts between the two contracting parties (Smith & Warner, 1979; Dichev & Skinner, 2002).

If debt covenants are meant to reduce agency conflicts between the borrower and the lender, then, their violation may constitute a highly source of costs for the breaching firm, as it can exacerbate the agency conflicts between the shareholders, the managers, and the bondholders, resulting in several undesired consequences for the corporate capital structure, such as a higher cost-of-capital, an increased level of financial distress, and a higher probability of bankruptcy (e.g., Roberts & Sufi, 2009; Gao et al., 2017; Freudenberg et al., 2017; Habib et al., 2020).

Aiming at avoiding such costly events, the managers may engage accounting discretion and other "window dressing" activities to obfuscate corporate's financial conditions and meet the lenders' requirements (e.g., Dyreng et al., 2022). Thanks to its effects on the after-tax cash flow, tax avoidance is likely to complement the set of strategies available to the managers to avoid or delay covenant violation, freeing up much needed cash resources to the company (Kim et al., 2010). However, scholars suggest that tax avoidance is not a simple transfer of resources from the state to the firm and its shareholders because of agency conflicts intrinsic into the managers-shareholders and bondholders' relationship (Desai & Dharmapala, 2009). Hence, the

A. Gabrielli, *Tax Avoidance and Capital Structure*, SIDREA Series in Accounting and Business Administration, https://doi.org/10.1007/978-3-031-30980-9_6

underlaying agency conflicts are likely affect the relationship between tax avoidance and debt covenant violation, as they can shape the reasons and motivation of the firm's tax reduction activities.

In this book, after having provided a broad overview on the role of taxes in the corporate capital structure theory, I start analyzing the implications of tax avoidance activities for a firm's capital structure in absence of agency considerations (see Chap. 2). According to this first stream of literature reviewed, firms use tax avoidance as an alternative source of financing through which to reduce the firm's cost of capital and its related risk of default. However, it has been argued that such a conclusion might be only partial if the agency costs pertaining to corporate capital structure decisions—including firm's tax avoidance decisions—are not considered.

In Chap. 3, the relationship between tax avoidance and capital structure is examined within an Agency perspective. The Agency Theory indicates that agency conflicts arise all the time in which two or more cooperating parties have different goals and a different set of information. Capital structure decisions are associated with significant conflicts of interests between the shareholders (and managers) and the bondholders. As a result, the final effect of tax avoidance on a firm's capital structure is likely to vary at different level of agency conflicts. Once introduced to the main channels by which tax avoidance activities can affect the corporate capital structure, Chap. 3 provides a special focus to the context of debt covenants, which, as anticipated, represent crucial feature of debt contracting for many firms and play a central role within a firm's capital structure management.

In Chap. 4, I provide an in-depth examination of the role of debt covenants in capital structure management as well as on the risk stemming from their violation. Furthermore, I discuss the main accounting strategies pursued by the managers to avoid or delay debt covenant violation. Basing on this literature, corporate tax avoidance is thus investigated as a potential strategy through which managers may attempt mitigating the debt covenant violation risk. Prior literature provided two competing views on the effect of tax avoidance for the debt covenant violation likelihood, predicting either a positive or negative effect (Kim et al., 2010; Hasan et al., 2014; Platikanova, 2017). According to certain studies, tax avoidance is not associated with agency conflicts and may provide additional cash resources useful to service corporate debt positions and enhance the firm's after-tax cash flow, thus reducing the risk of debt covenant violation (Kim et al., 2010; Lim, 2011; Lin et al., 2014). Conversely, other studies suggest that tax avoidance activities are intimately tied with agency conflicts and may be related to a higher covenant violation likelihood, owing to higher future cash flow uncertainty, financial reporting opacity, reputational risks, and potential opportunism and discretion by the managers on the use of corporate resources (Hasan et al., 2014; Platikanova, 2017; Dhawan et al., 2020).

The life cycle literature suggests that agency conflicts are heterogenous across a firm life cycle and advocates for further research on tax avoidance activities across the life cycle stages of a firm (Hasan et al., 2017; Habib & Hasan, 2019). Recent scholarship indicates that the firm's transition across its life cycle stages does not depend on firm's age but rather on its cash flow patterns (Dickinson, 2011; Hasan et al., 2017). Jensen (1986) argues that corporate cash flow patterns (i.e., level of free cash flow available) may provide parsimonious information on the level of agency conflicts between the managers, the shareholders, and on the related monitoring advantage that is expected from debt. Hence, the level of agency conflicts (and the related agency benefit of debt) is expected to vary across the different life cycle stages (Vos & Forlong, 1996; Habib & Hasan, 2019). Basing on these considerations, Chap. 4 ends providing a set of hypotheses that relate tax avoidance with the debt covenant violation likelihood at each stage of the corporate life cycle.

Finally, in Chap. 5, the book empirically tests the hypotheses set at Chap. 4, by investigating a large sample of U.S. public firms. Specifically, the research answer the research question of whether the relationship between tax avoidance and debt covenant violation is contingent to the life cycle stage the firm is in. As said, life cycle stages are associated to specific cash flow patterns and reflect different level of alignment of interests between the managers and the shareholders (Jensen, 1986; Dickinson, 2011). The empirical findings support the hypotheses.

Overall, this book can add to prior tax literature in several new and original ways. First, this study can add to the Agency Theory of tax avoidance, by suggesting the centrality of the free cash flow and related life cycle-contingent cash flow patterns in explaining the implications of tax avoidance for a firm's capital structure. Although the book primarily focuses on debt covenant violation as a real event affecting the capital structure management of many firms, much of the theoretical considerations developed can plausibly be extended to other capital structure contingencies such as, the cost-of-capital, the default likelihood, and the risk of financial distress (Habib et al., 2020). In this sense, the research can offer an original, theoretically grounded, reconciliation of two competing Agency Theory-based views (i.e., the "tunneling view" and the "value-enhancing" view) regarding the effect of tax avoidance for the corporate capital structure, as emerged from prior literature.

Second, the research adds to the empirical literature investigating the consequences of tax avoidance for the debt covenants. Prior literature predicted conflicting views on the association between tax avoidance and debt covenant violation (Kim et al., 2010; Hasan et al., 2014; Platikanova, 2017). According to Kim et al. (2010), banks are willing to impose fewer covenant restrictions to aggressive tax avoider firms as they are less likely to violate covenants' terms. Conversely, other studies suggest that tax avoider firms are more likely to incur covenant violations and are burdened, on average, by more stringent financial conditions (e.g., Hasan et al., 2014; Platikanova, 2017). This study complements this stream of research showing that the effect of tax avoidance on the debt covenant violation likelihood is contingent to the life cycle stage of a firm. Specifically, introductory and decline tax avoider firms are more likely to reduce their covenant violation likelihood when engaging higher level of tax avoidance. Conversely, for firms in the mature stage, tax avoidance is likely to increase the risk of violation, possibly due to a higher uncertainty on future cash flow, a higher financial reporting opacity, reputational risks, and managerial discretion associated to the use of corporate resources.

Third, this study can also provide useful insights to the stream of tax literature that builds on the debt-tax avoidance substitution hypothesis to examine the relationship between tax avoidance, the cost of capital, and the related risk of default (e.g., Lim, 2011; Richardson et al., 2014). Prior literature argues that a higher level of tax avoidance is expected to be associated with a lower cost of capital and a lower risk of default because it lowers the amount of outstanding debt, due to the debt substitution effect. This study suggests that, due to the substitution effect, a higher level of tax avoidance can be expected to increase to increase the cost of capital, the likelihood of debt covenant violation, and the related risk of default, if the marginal agency benefits of debt outweigh the agency costs of debt. In this way, this study caution researchers to consider the potential reduction of the agency benefits of debt (as induced by the substitution effect), when interpreting the results of their research.

Finally, this book provides a review of main theories and empirical evidence on the effect of tax avoidance on the cost of capital and the related interacting effect exerted by agency conflicts. By shedding lights on the on the potential effects of tax avoidance on the firm's capital structure, it is hope that this book could be of interest for both experienced and early-stage scholars interested in the topic, as well as for investors, analysts, lenders, and other market participants. The results of the research can also be useful to orientate policymakers and regulatory agencies.

6.2   Potential Avenues for Future Research

The recent economic instability triggered by the Covid-19 crisis has prompt many policymakers and regulators to adopt several initiatives and public spending measures with the aim to support businesses' operating stability and to avoid financial disruptions (Baldwin & Weder di Mauro, 2020; De Vito & Gómez, 2020). Goodell (2020) suggests that the recent Covid-19 pandemic is likely to permanently change firms' financing and to determining a long-term impact on firms' capital structure. In time of crisis, more than ever, the joint consideration of tax issues and the sustainability of the cost of the capital structure is deemed crucial (Brondolo, 2009). Recent empirical research suggests that financially constrained firms potentially source for funds obtained through cash savings generated through tax avoidance activities (Richardson et al., 2015; Law & Mills, 2015; Edwards et al., 2016). Other studies also find that firms change their capital structure choices as a response to changes to the external environment, for example by pursuing conservative debt policies (Huang et al., 2020; Elnahas et al., 2018). While an existing stream of research has already investigated the implication of tax avoidance for a firm's capital structure, there is limited knowledge on whether and how such relationship could change in the presence of external macroeconomic and/or environmental shocks. For example, future research could address the following research question: Did tax avoidance help firms to recover their pre-pandemic capital structure choices in the aftermath of the Covid-19 crisis? How the structure of tax incentives employed during the pandemic has modified the firms' choices and cost of capital structure? Exploiting the setting provided by the Covid-19 crisis through appropriate quasi-experimental research studies could be of interest not only to early inform the current academic debate but also to address endogeneity issues implicitly associated to the research questions.

Moreover, since agency conflicts between managers and shareholders are relevant in influencing a firm's tax minimization decisions, another interesting aspect could be to broaden the investigation of the capital structure to all the forms of tax planning. In a recent paper, Schwab et al. (2022) developed a new measure that can help to capture effective tax planning. Effective tax planning is described as the firm's ability to maximize its after-tax returns given the level of pre-tax income, research and development expenditures, intangible assets, interest expense, and capital intensity. This measure, according to the authors, can better reflect the traditional Scholes and Wolfson's definition of tax planning, according to which effective tax planning does not only consist in explicit tax minimization (i.e., tax avoidance), but—more broadly—in the joint consideration of "all parties", "all taxes", and "all costs" implicated in a certain business transaction (including implicit taxes minimization). Future research could use the new proxy developed by Schwab et al. (2022) to investigate how often corporate tax minimization activities collide with an optimal (i.e., "effective") tax planning and whether the level of free cash flow (i.e., agency conflicts) can help understanding cross-sectional differences in firms' tax planning activities and their implication for a firm's cost of capital structure.

There is also an emerging line of research that examines the role of managerial ability on tax planning decisions and corporate tax avoidance. Koester et al. (2017) suggest that the minimization of income tax payments and the way such minimization is achieved is determined by the management's ability: firms with higher-ability managers make higher use of tax havens, R&D tax claims, and engage in greater investment to generate accelerate depreciation deductions with respect to firms with lower management's ability. Khurana et al. (2018) find that the effect of tax avoidance on investment efficiency is also moderated by the firm's managerial activity. Similarly, Kubick et al. (2020) find that the presence of "tax-savvy" executives (i.e., managers with significant professional tax experiences) is positively associated with lower effective tax rates. Future studies can investigate whether managerial ability affects the trade-off between debt and tax avoidance decisions, and its impact on the firms' cost of capital structure and default likelihood.

To date, there is also scant empirical knowledge regarding the debt-monitoring hypothesis (a.k.a., agency benefits of debt) and how this could affect a firm's tax avoidance behaviour. This lack of knowledge is presumably related to the difficulty in finding suitable proxies for the agency benefits of debt. Previous studies predominately focused on the agency costs of debt (e.g., bankruptcy costs, asset substitution). Nonetheless, some papers have also attempted an empirical investigation of the agency benefits of debt (e.g., Zantout, 1997; Gul & Tsui, 1997, 2001; Griffin et al., 2010). In this respect, a related interesting new avenue for future research is that one examining the role of inside debt on a firm's tax avoidance decisions. Alexander and Pisa (2021) provide early evidence of a credit market generated disciplining effect on tax avoidance, showing that firms with refencing needs may prefer to forego certain tax avoidance opportunities in order to gain their future access to bank credit, especially during adverse credit market conditions. Alexander and Jacob (2016) also find as an explanation for the observed cross-sectional differences in firm's tax avoidance behaviour the presence of executives inside debt. Future studies can extend this literature by investigating, for example, whether different types of indebtment are associated with higher or lower tax avoidance. Moreover, future empirical research can draw on the free cash flow hypothesis (Jensen, 1986) and on the debt substitution hypothesis (DeAngelo & Masulis, 1980) to examine the association between tax avoidance and optimal leverage. Specifically, the following research questions could be addressed by future research: does deviation from optimal leverage ratio explain the effect of tax avoidance on the cost of capital structure? does tax avoidance activities affects the capital structure's speed of adjustment?

Finally, following the seminal works of Jensen (1976, 1986, 1989), agency theorists have started to enlarge the plethora of subjects to be considered when developing agency frameworks. For example, Hill and Jones (1992) developed an agency framework that goes beyond the traditional managers-shareholders and bondholders' conflict, ending for including other stakeholders such as, workers, suppliers, external agencies, and the public community. In this respect, future studies could exploit different sources of cross-sectional variation in the level agency conflicts to examine the relationship between tax avoidance and capital structure. Since the structure of equity ownership is an important aspect affecting the agency conflict between shareholders and managers, a particularly promising avenue of investigation could be that one of family business. For example, Anderson et al. (2003) examine the effect of founding family ownership on a firm's cost of debt, showing that firms with substantial family ownership stake are more prone to mitigate agency conflicts with debtholders, thus bearing a lower cost of debt when re-entering the debt market. This result could suggest that family firms are more likely to choose more debt and less tax avoidance as a source of financing, since additional debt is more likely to be associate with a reduction of the agency conflicts between the shareholders and the managers. However, there is still no conclusive evidence in the family business literature on the relationship between agency conflicts and tax avoidance nor of its relationship with the cost-of-capital. For example, Chen et al. (2010) finds lower tax aggressiveness in family firms, consistent with family firms foregoing certain tax minimization opportunities. Chen et al. (2010) attribute this result to the unique agency conflict affecting family firms: the conflict between dominant shareholders (i.e., family owners) and the minority shareholders (i.e., non-family owners).[1] Badertscher et al. (2019) starts by replicating Chen et al. (2010), confirming that family ownership is associated with lower tax avoidance when measured by non-conforming tax rates. However, they do not find a similar association when measured as conforming tax avoidance, which, in contrast, is found to higher in family firms. Future research can investigate whether and how

---

[1] This conflict is also known as "principal-principal conflict".

family ownership affects the debt-tax avoidance substitution and its implication on the firm's cost of capital structure.

References

Alexander, A., & Jacob, M. (2016). *Executive inside debt and corporate tax avoidance*.

Alexander, A., & Pisa, M. (2021). *Credit refinancing and corporate tax avoidance*. Available at SSRN 3774085.

Anderson, R. C., Mansi, S. A., & Reeb, D. M. (2003). Founding family ownership and the agency cost of debt. *Journal of Financial Economics, 68*(2), 263–285.

Badertscher, B. A., Katz, S. P., Rego, S. O., & Wilson, R. J. (2019). Conforming tax avoidance and capital market pressure. *The Accounting Review, 94*(6), 1–30.

Baldwin, R., & Weder di Mauro, B. (2020). *Mitigating the COVID economic crisis: Act fast and do whatever it takes*. VoxEU.org. CEPR Press. Available at: https://voxeu.org/content/mitigating-covid-economic-crisis-act-fast-and-do-whatever-it-takes

Brondolo, J. (2009). *Collecting taxes during an economic crisis: Challenges and policy options*. IMF Staff Position Notes 2009(017).

Chen, S., Chen, X., Cheng, Q., & Shevlin, T. (2010). Are family firms more tax aggressive than non-family firms? *Journal of Financial Economics, 95*(1), 41–61.

De Vito, A., & Gómez, J.-P. (2020). Estimating the COVID-19 cash crunch: Global evidence and policy. *Journal of Accounting and Public Policy, 39*(2), 106741.

DeAngelo, H., & Masulis, R. W. (1980). Leverage and dividend irrelevancy under corporate and personal taxation. *The Journal of Finance, 35*(2), 453–464.

Demerjian, P. R., & Owens, E. L. (2016). Measuring the probability of financial covenant violation in private debt contracts. *Journal of Accounting and Economics, 61*(2–3), 433–447.

Desai, M. A., & Dharmapala, D. (2009). Corporate tax avoidance and firm value. *The Review of Economics and Statistics, 91*(3), 537–546.

Dhawan, A., Ma, L., & Kim, M. H. (2020). Effect of corporate tax avoidance activities on firm bankruptcy risk. *Journal of Contemporary Accounting & Economics, 16*(2), 100187.

Dichev, I. D., & Skinner, D. J. (2002). Large–Sample evidence on the debt covenant hypothesis. *Journal of Accounting Research, 40*(4), 1091–1123.

Dickinson, V. (2011). Cash flow patterns as a proxy for firm life cycle. *The Accounting Review, 86* (6), 1969–1994.

Dyreng, S. D., Hillegeist, S. A., & Penalva, F. (2022). Earnings management to avoid debt covenant violations and future performance. *European Accounting Review, 31*(2), 311–343.

Edwards, A., Schwab, C., & Shevlin, T. (2016). Financial constraints and cash tax savings. *The Accounting Review, 91*(3), 859–881.

Elnahas, A., Kim, D., & Kim, I. (2018). *Natural disaster risk and corporate leverage*. Available at SSRN 3123468.

Freudenberg, F., Imbierowicz, B., Saunders, A., & Steffen, S. (2017). Covenant violations and dynamic loan contracting. *Journal of Corporate Finance, 45*, 540–565.

Gao, Y., Khan, M., & Tan, L. (2017). Further evidence on consequences of debt covenant violations. *Contemporary Accounting Research, 34*(3), 1489–1521.

Goodell, J. W. (2020). COVID-19 and finance: Agendas for future research. *Finance Research Letters, 35*, 101512.

Griffin, P. A., Lont, D. H., & Sun, Y. (2010). Agency problems and audit fees: Further tests of the free cash flow hypothesis. *Accounting and Finance, 50*(2), 321–350.

Gul, F. A., & Tsui, J. S. L. (1997). A test of the free cash flow and debt monitoring hypotheses: Evidence from audit pricing. *Journal of Accounting and Economics, 24*(2), 219–237.

Gul, F. A., & Tsui, J. S. (2001). Free cash flow, debt monitoring, and audit pricing: Further evidence on the role of director equity ownership. *Auditing: A Journal of Practice and Theory, 20*(2), 71–84.

Habib, A., Costa, M. D., Huang, H. J., Bhuiyan, M. B. U., & Sun, L. (2020). Determinants and consequences of financial distress: review of the empirical literature. *Accounting and Finance, 60*, 1023–1075.

Habib, A., & Hasan, M. M. (2019). Corporate life cycle research in accounting, finance and corporate governance: A survey, and directions for future research. *International Review of Financial Analysis, 61(C)*, 188–201.

Hasan, M. M., Al-Hadi, A., Taylor, G., & Richardson, G. (2017). Does a firm's life cycle Explain its propensity to engage in corporate tax avoidance? *European Accounting Review, 26*(3), 469–501. https://doi.org/10.1080/09638180.2016.1194220

Hasan, I., Hoi, C. K. S., Wu, Q., & Zhang, H. (2014). Beauty is in the eye of the beholder: The effect of corporate tax avoidance on the cost of bank loans. *Journal of Financial Economics, 113*(1), 109–130.

Hill, C. W., & Jones, T. M. (1992). Stakeholder-agency theory. *Journal of Management Studies, 29*(2), 131–154.

Huang, Z., Gao, W., & Chen, L. (2020). Does the external environment matter for the persistence of firms' debt policy? *Finance Research Letters, 32*, 101073.

Jensen, M. C. (1986). Agency costs of free cash flow, corporate finance, and takeovers. *The American Economic Review, 76*, 323–329. https://doi.org/10.2139/ssrn.99580

Jensen, M. C. (1989). Active investors, LBOs, and the privatization of bankruptcy. *Journal of Applied Corporate Finance, 2*(1), 35–44.

Jensen, M. C., & Meckling, W. H. (1976). Theory of the firm: Managerial behavior, agency costs and ownership structure. *Journal of Financial Economics, 3*(4), 305–360.

Khurana, I. K., Moser, W. J., & Raman, K. K. (2018). Tax avoidance, managerial ability, and investment efficiency. *Abacus, 54*(4), 547–575.

Kim, J. B., Li, O. Z., & Li, Y. (2010). *Corporate tax avoidance and bank loan contracting.* Working paper, City University of Hong Kong, National University of Singapore, and Arizona State University. Available at SSRN 1596209.

Koester, A., Shevlin, T., & Wangerin, D. (2017). The role of managerial ability in corporate tax avoidance. *Management Science, 63*(10), 3285–3310.

Kubick, T. R., Li, Y., & Robinson, J. R. (2020). Tax-savvy executives. *Review of Accounting Studies, 25*(4), 1301–1343.

Law, K. K., & Mills, L. F. (2015). Taxes and financial constraints: Evidence from linguistic cues. *Journal of Accounting Research, 53*(4), 777–819.

Lim, Y. (2011). Tax avoidance, cost of debt and shareholder activism: Evidence from Korea. *Journal of Banking and Finance, 35*(2), 456–470.

Lin, S., Tong, N., & Tucker, A. L. (2014). Corporate tax aggression and debt. *Journal of Banking and Finance, 40*, 227–241.

Platikanova, P. (2017). Debt maturity and tax avoidance. *European Accounting Review, 26*(1), 97–124.

Richardson, G., Lanis, R., & Leung, S. C. M. (2014). Corporate tax aggressiveness, outside directors, and debt policy: An empirical analysis. *Journal of Corporate Finance, 25*, 107–121.

Roberts, M. R., & Sufi, A. (2009). Control rights and capital structure: An empirical investigation. *The Journal of Finance, 64*(4), 1657–1695.

Schwab, C. M., Stomberg, B., & Williams, B. M. (2022). Effective tax planning. *The Accounting Review, 97*(1), 413–437.

Smith, C. W., Jr., & Warner, J. B. (1979). On financial contracting: An analysis of bond covenants. *Journal of Financial Economics, 7*(2), 117–161.

Vos, E., & Forlong, C. (1996). The agency advantage of debt over the lifecycle of the firm. *The Journal of Entrepreneurial Finance, 5*(3), 193–211.

Zantout, Z. Z. (1997). A test of the debt-monitoring hypothesis: The case of corporate R&D expenditures. *Financial Review, 32*(1), 21–48.